...
Rumi

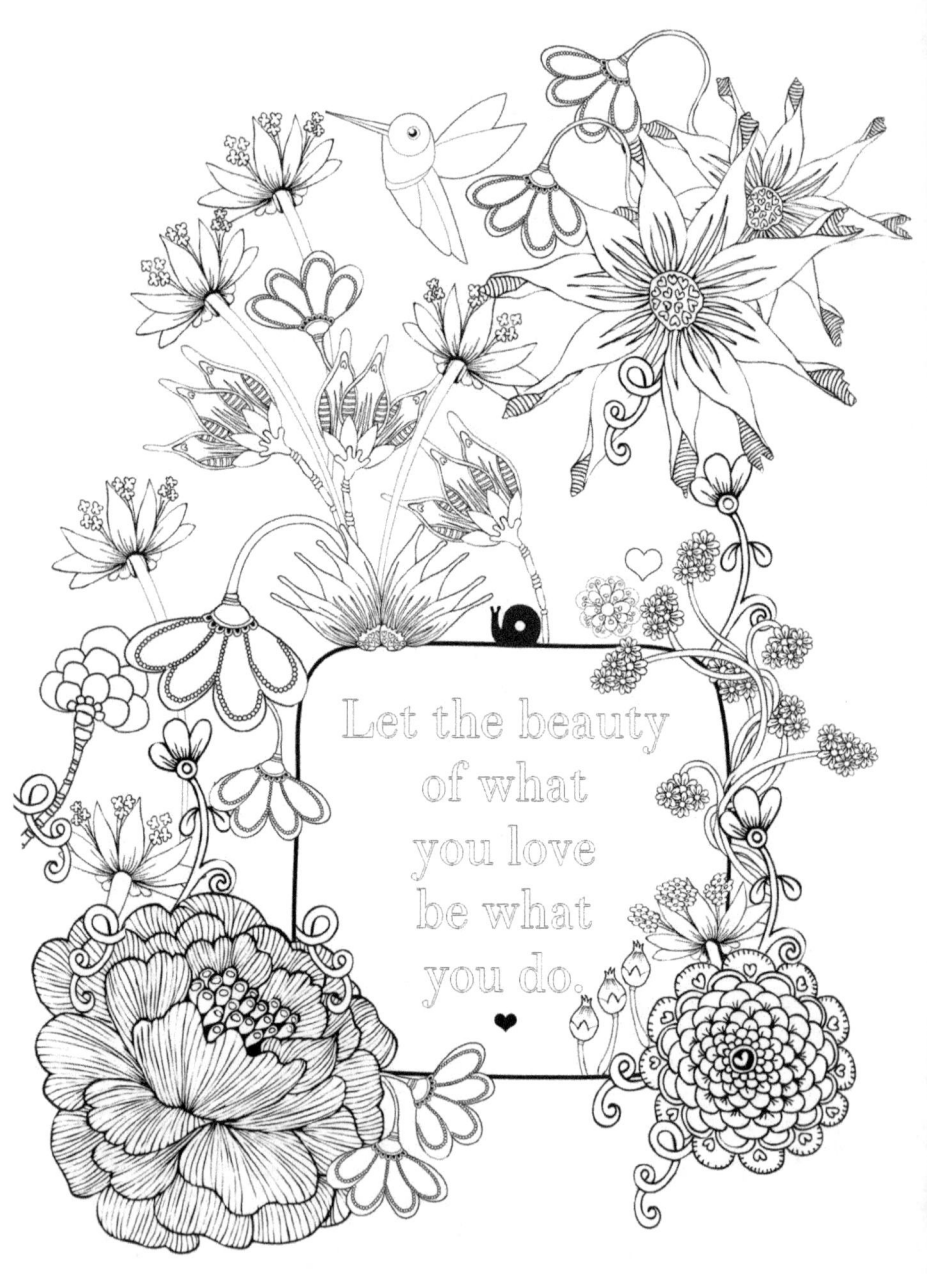

...
Rumi

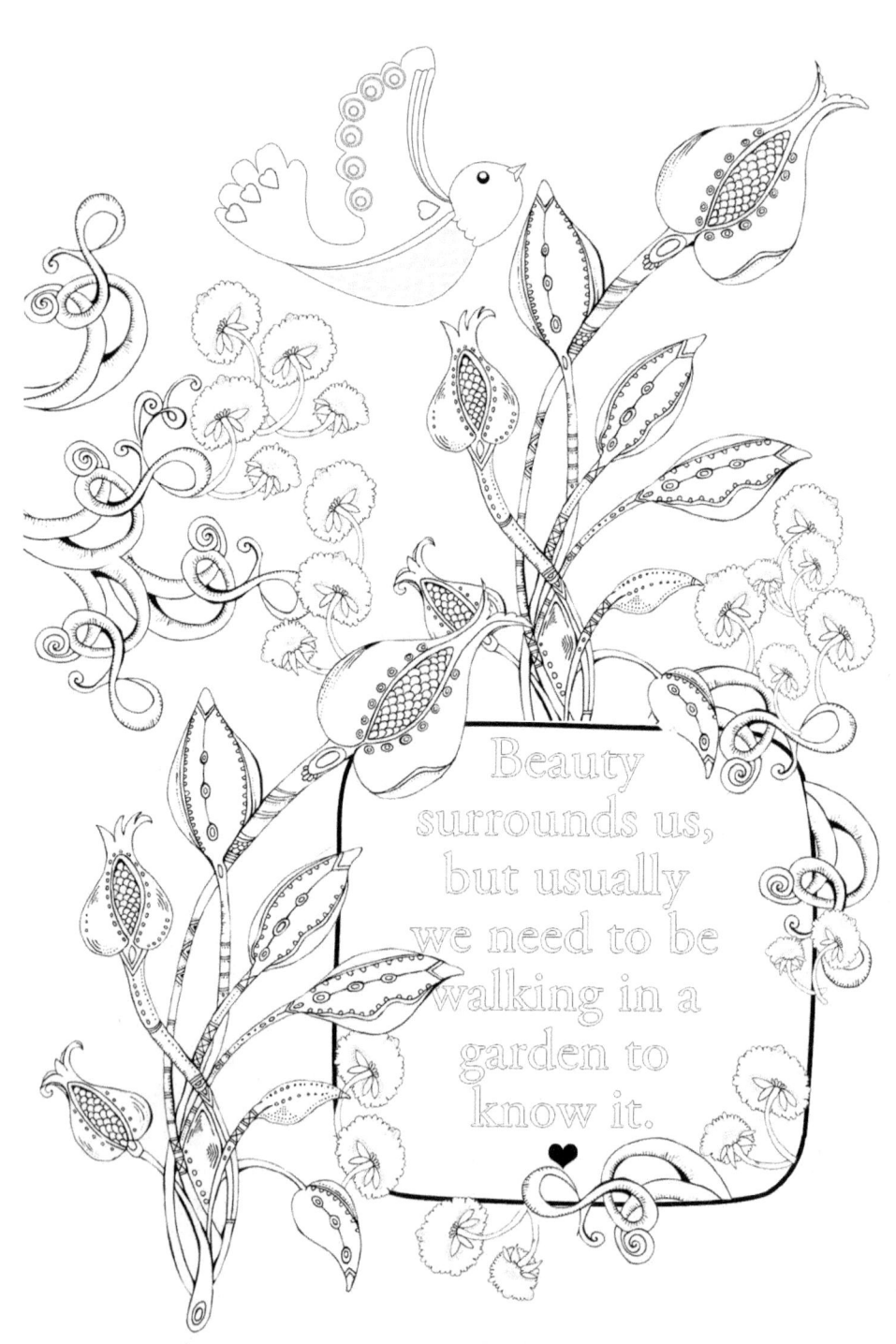

...
Rumi

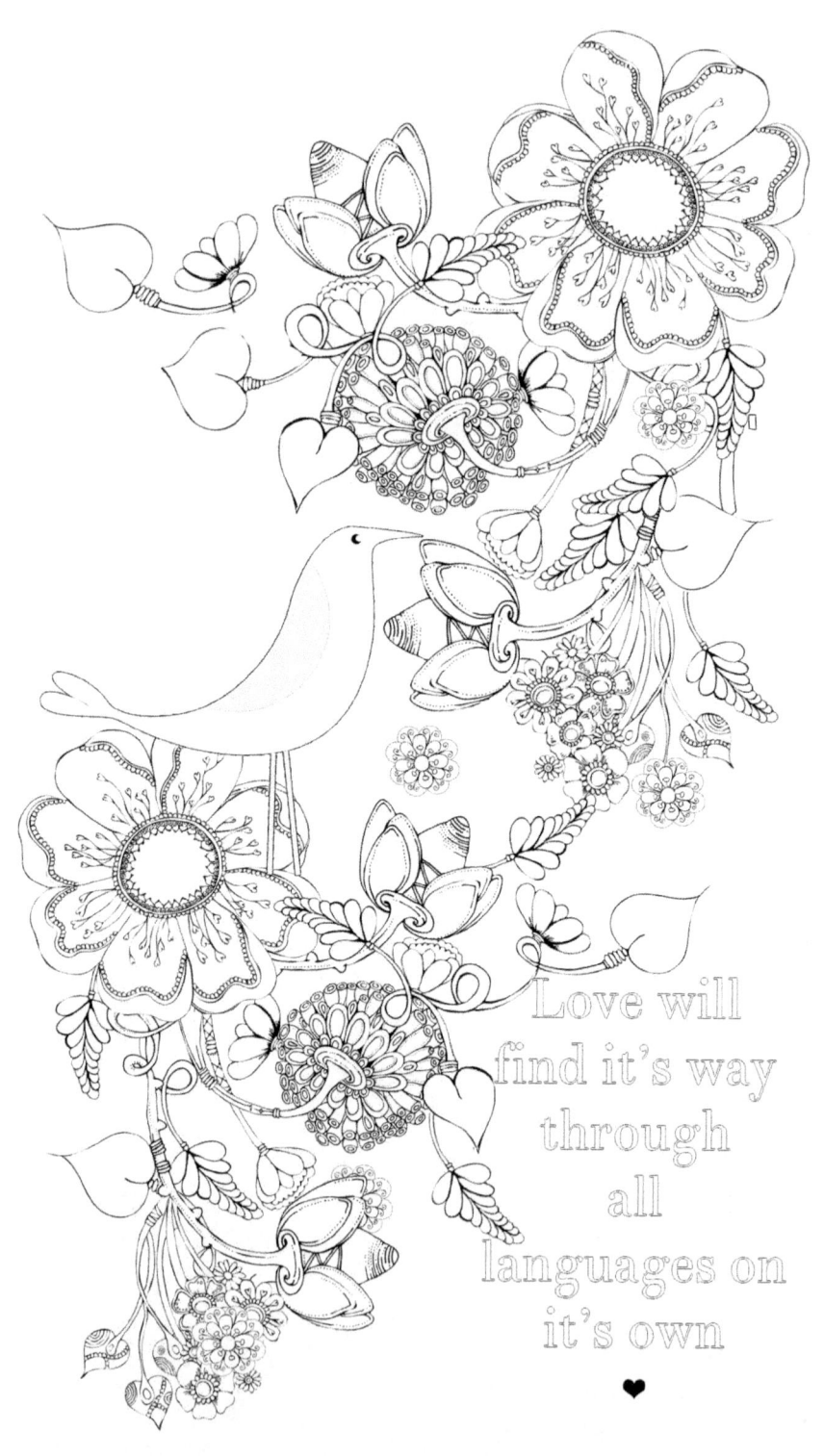

...
Rumi

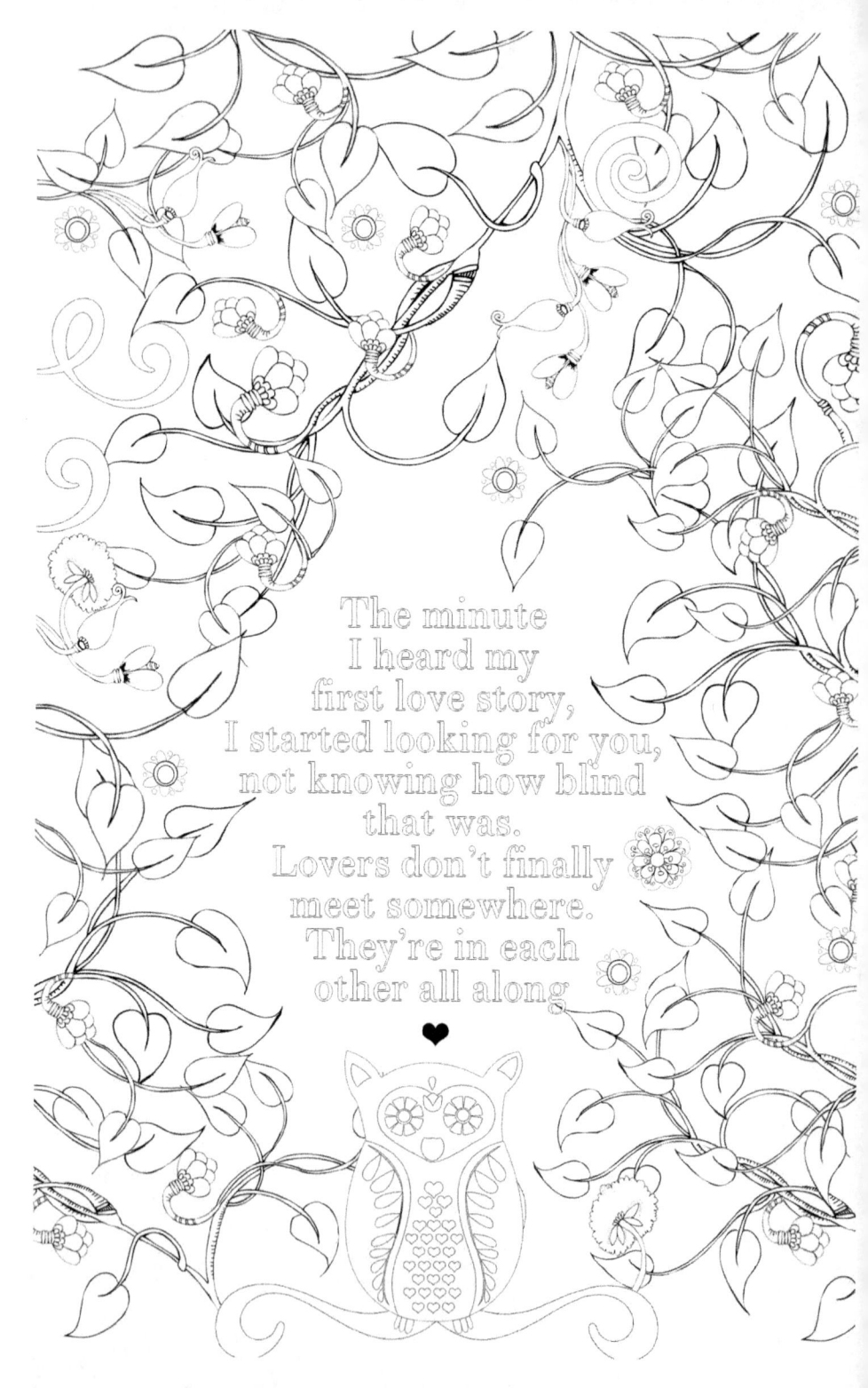

...
Rumi

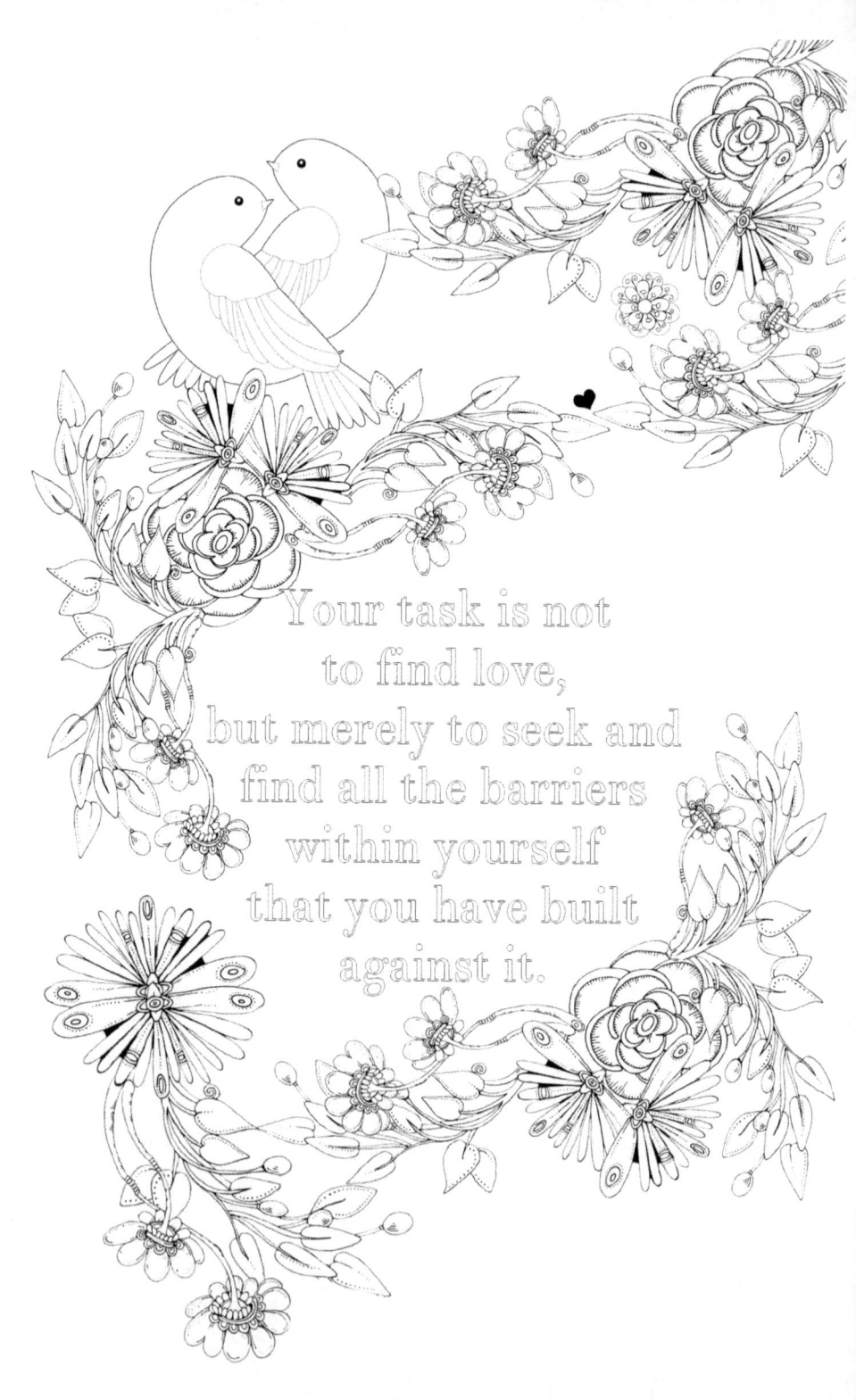

Your task is not
to find love,
but merely to seek and
find all the barriers
within yourself
that you have built
against it.

...
Rumi

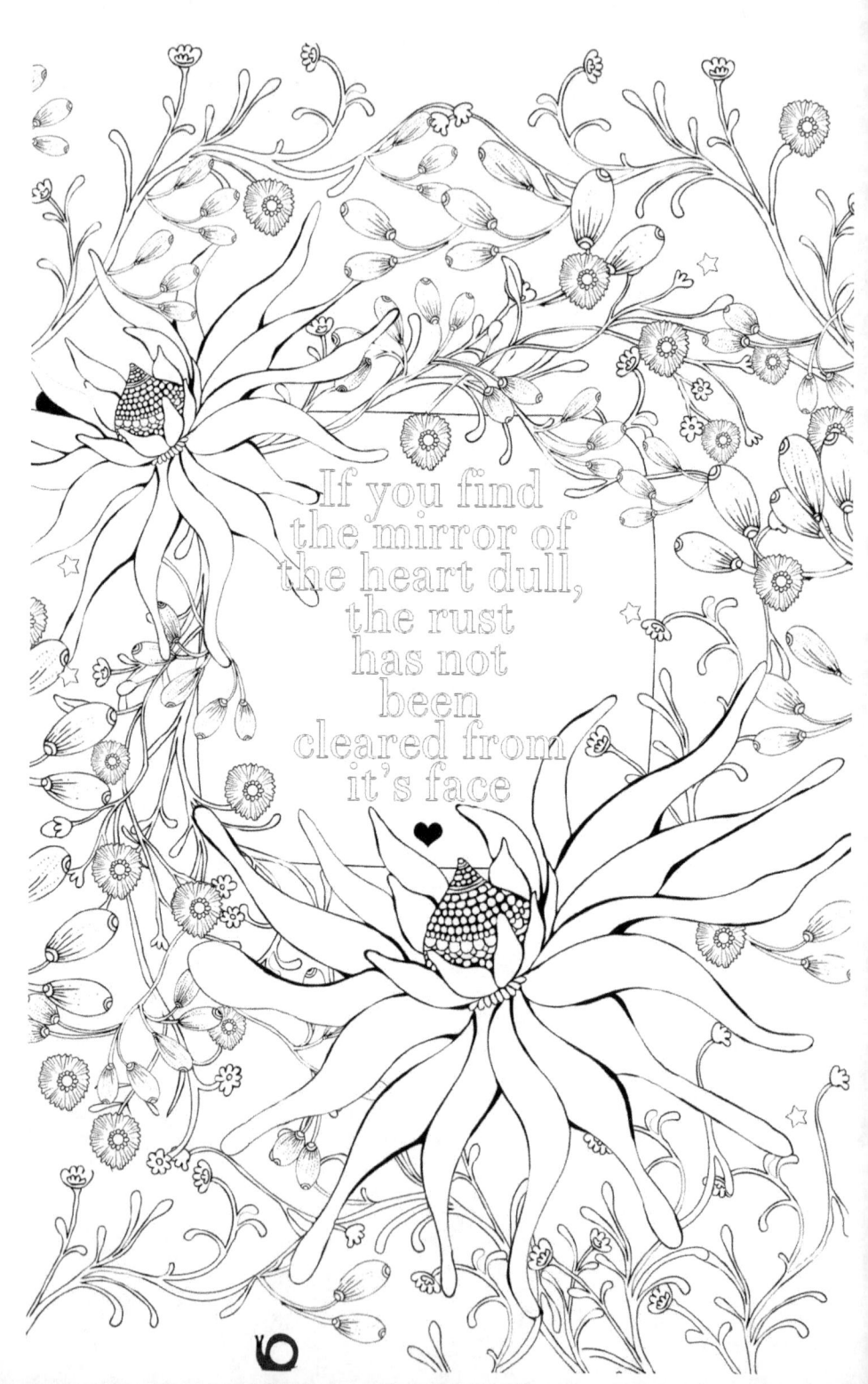

...
Rumi

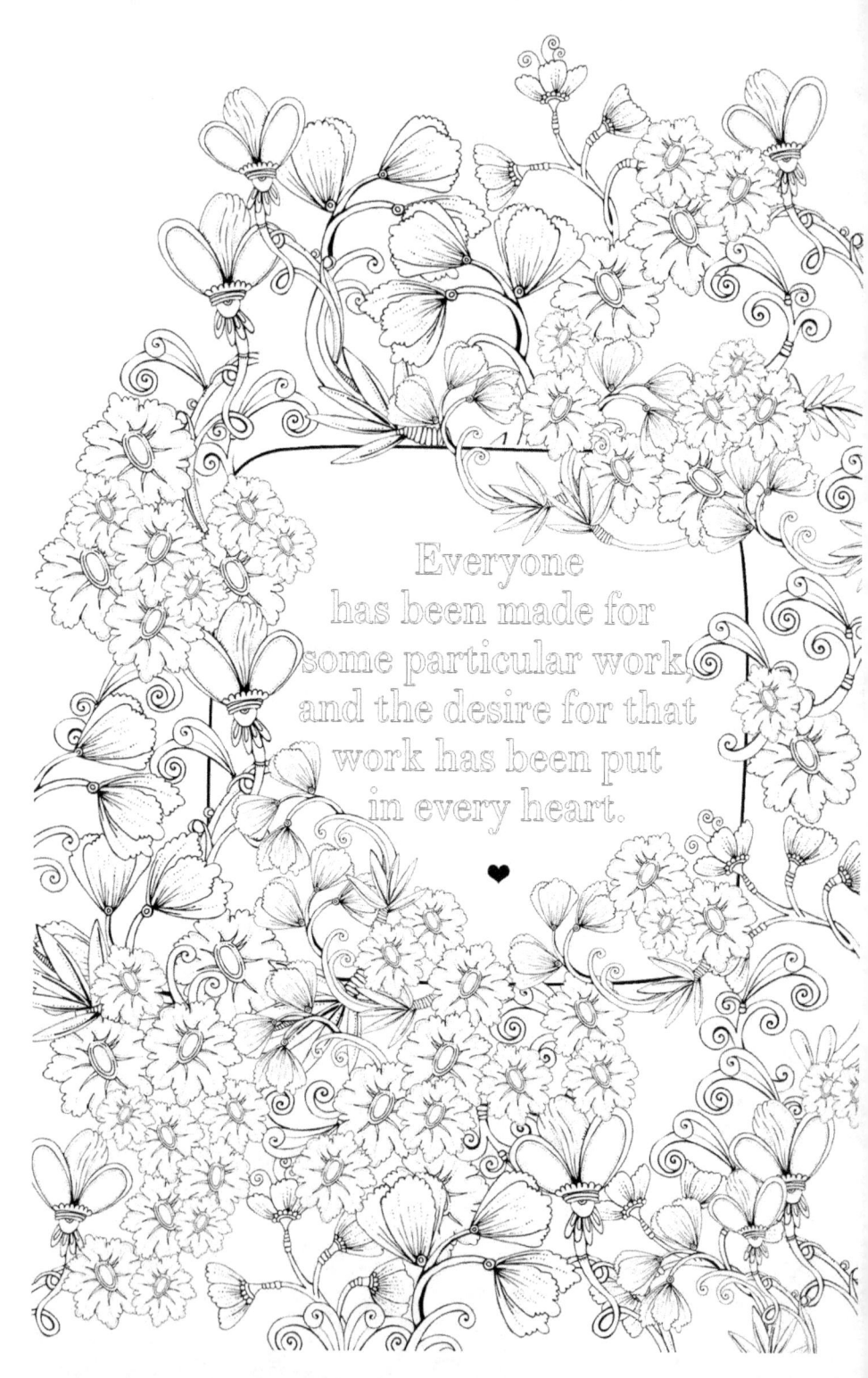

Rumi

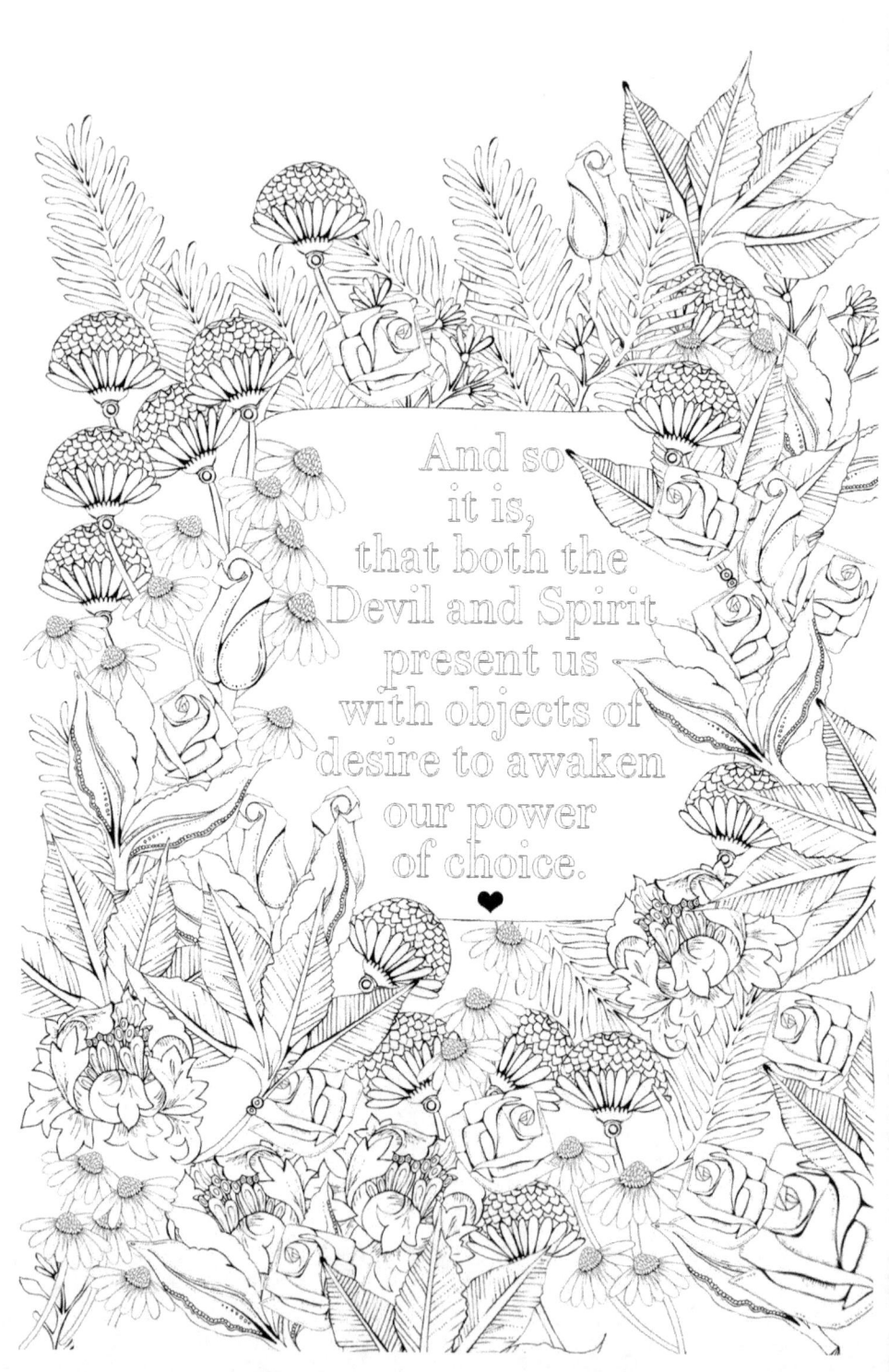

...
Rumi

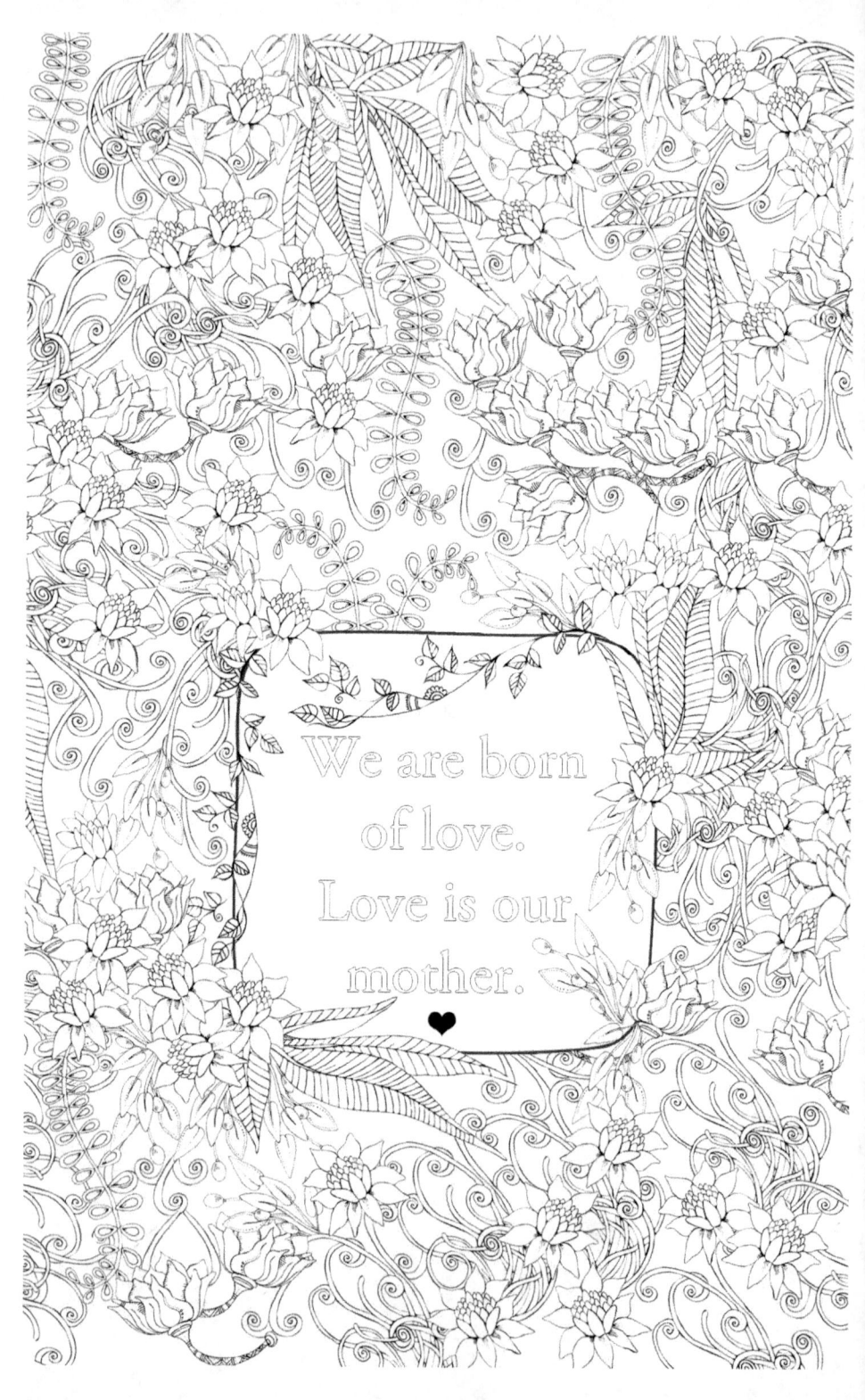

...
Rumi

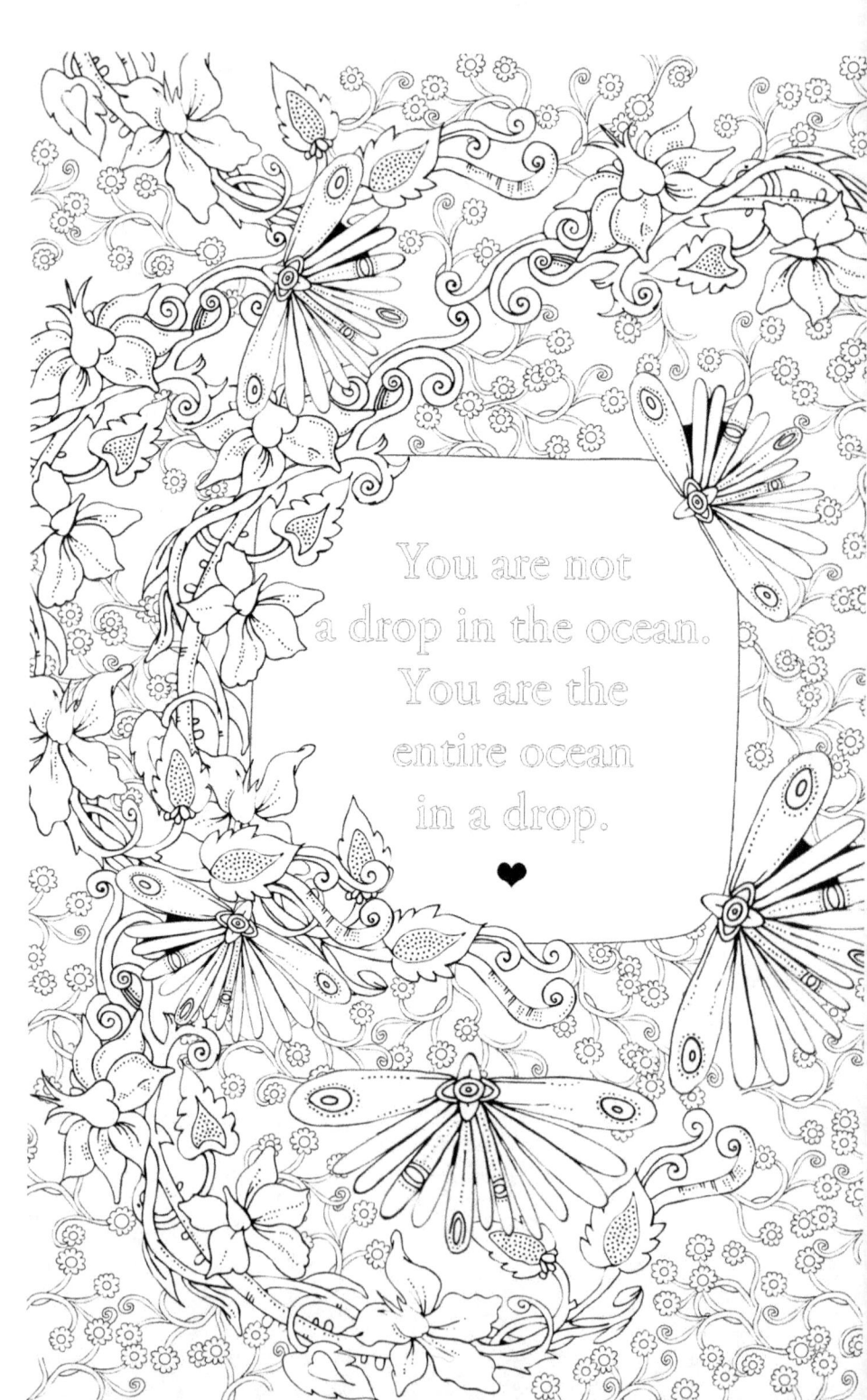

Rumi

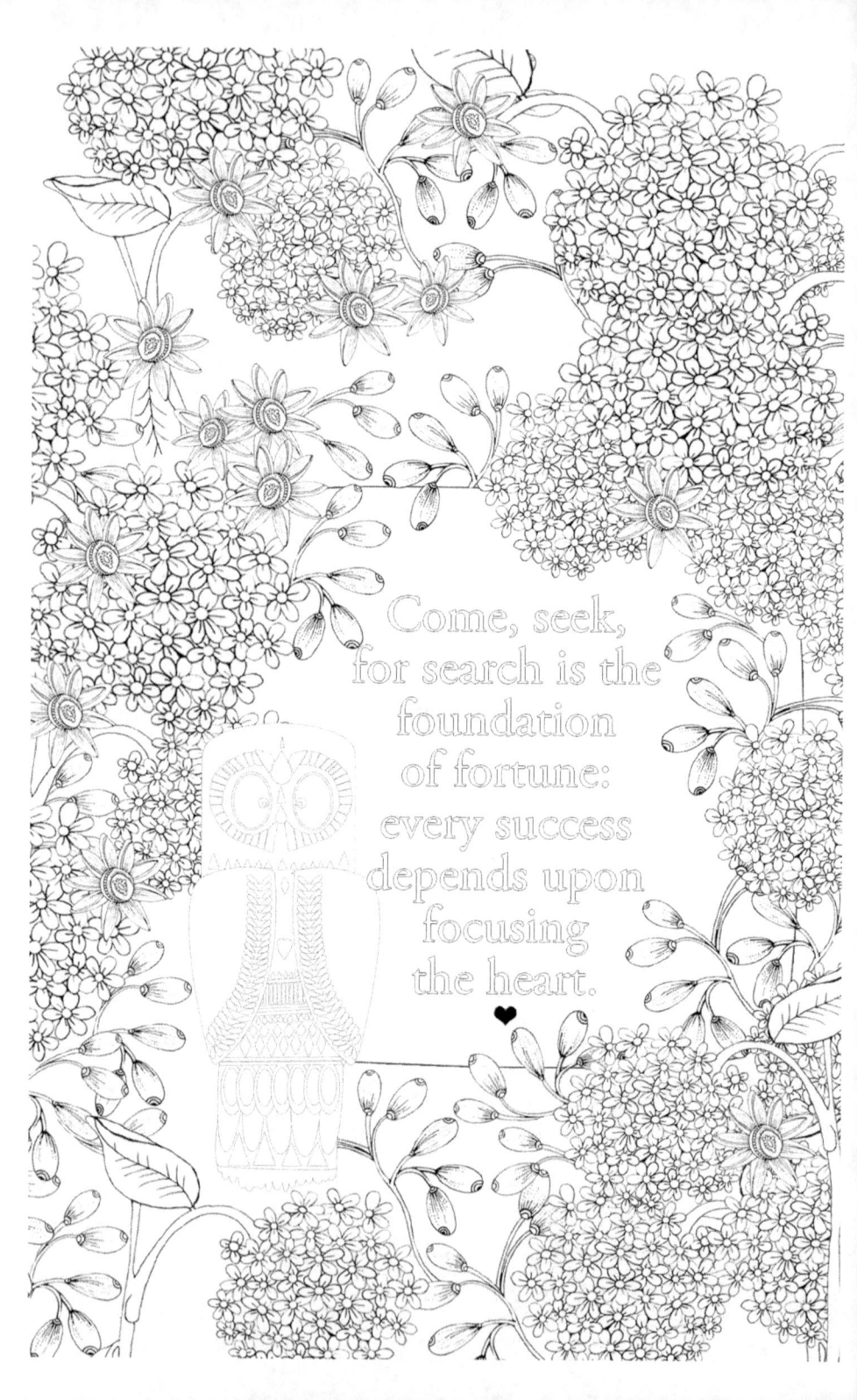

Rumi

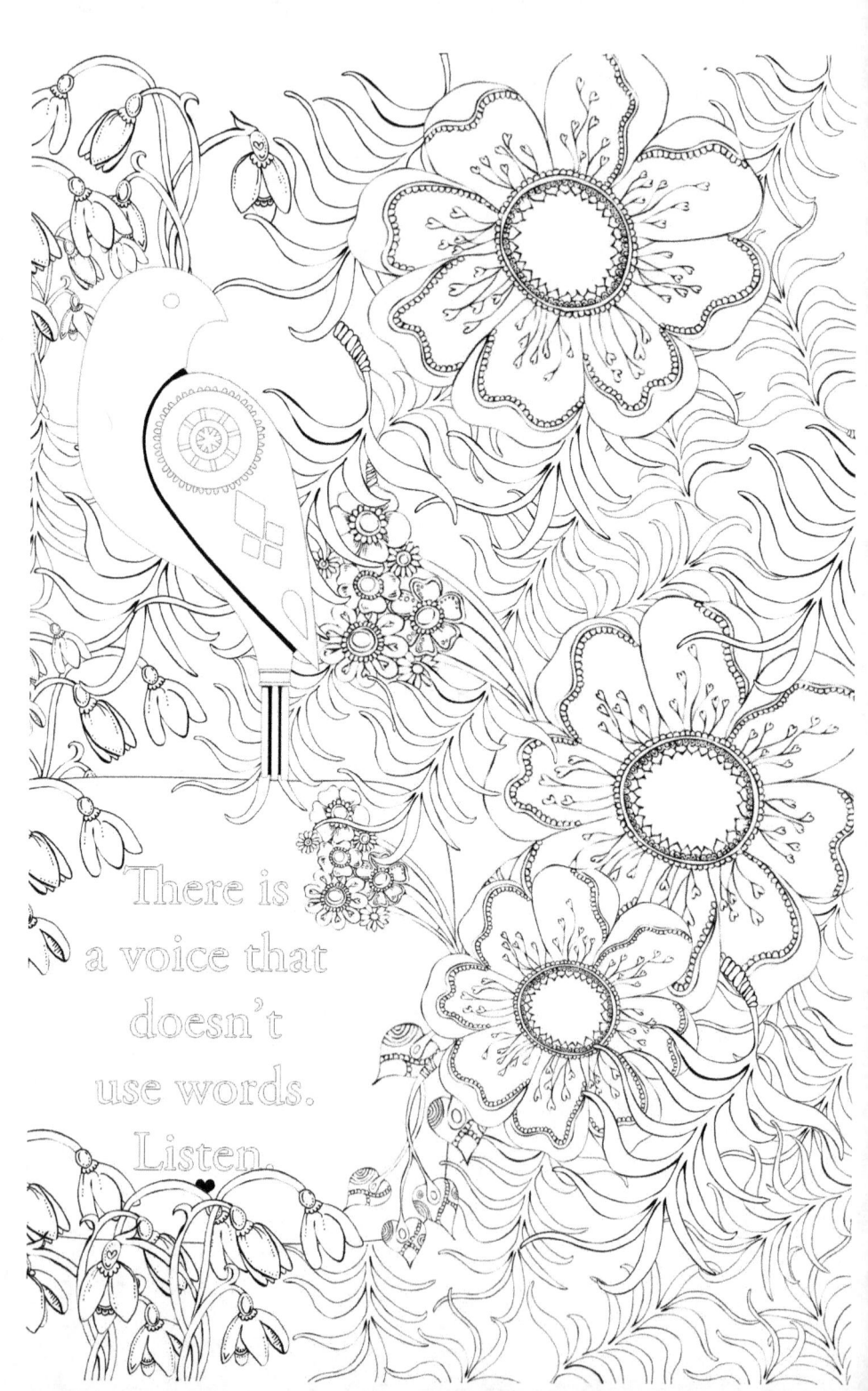

...
Rumi

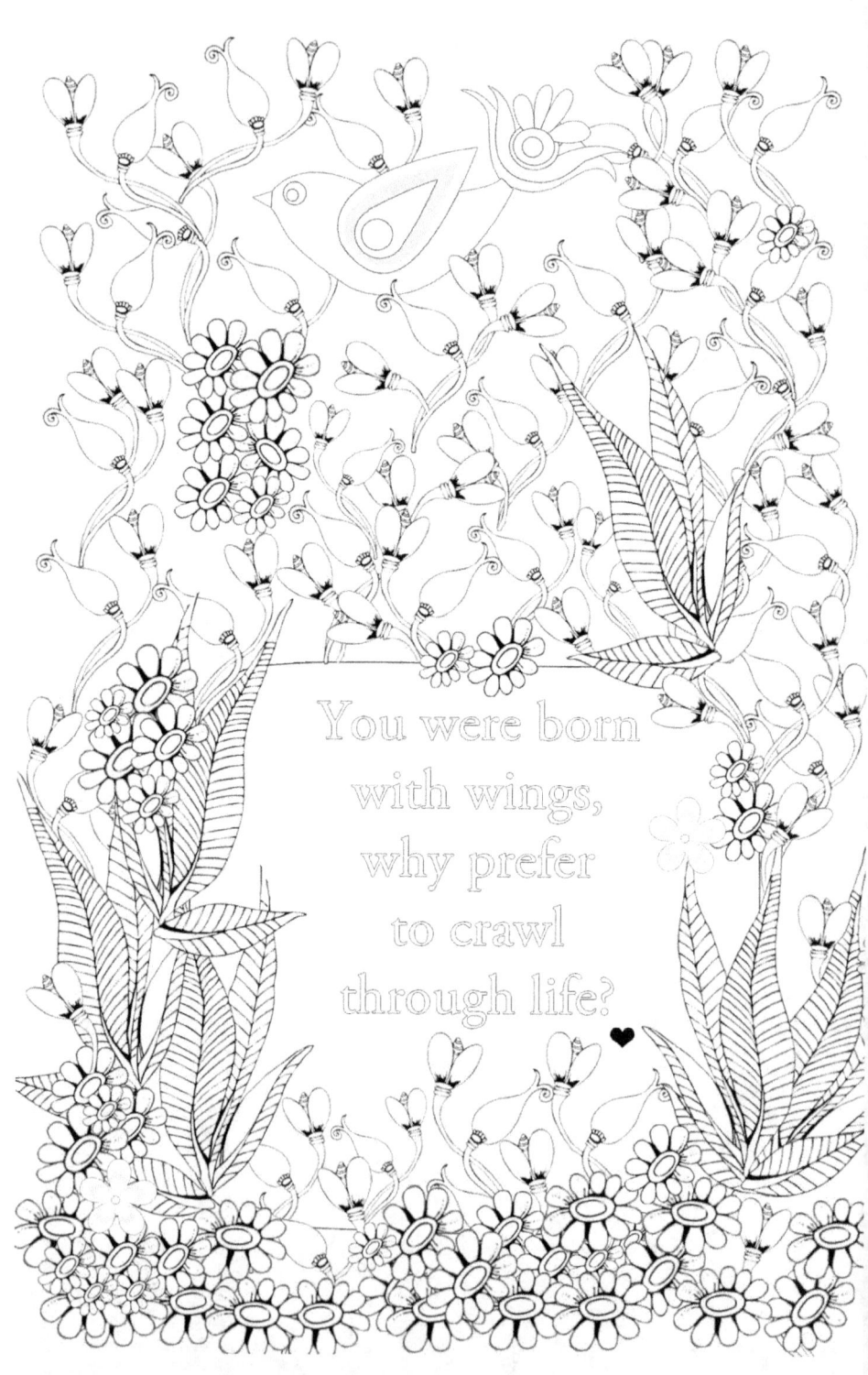

...
Rumi

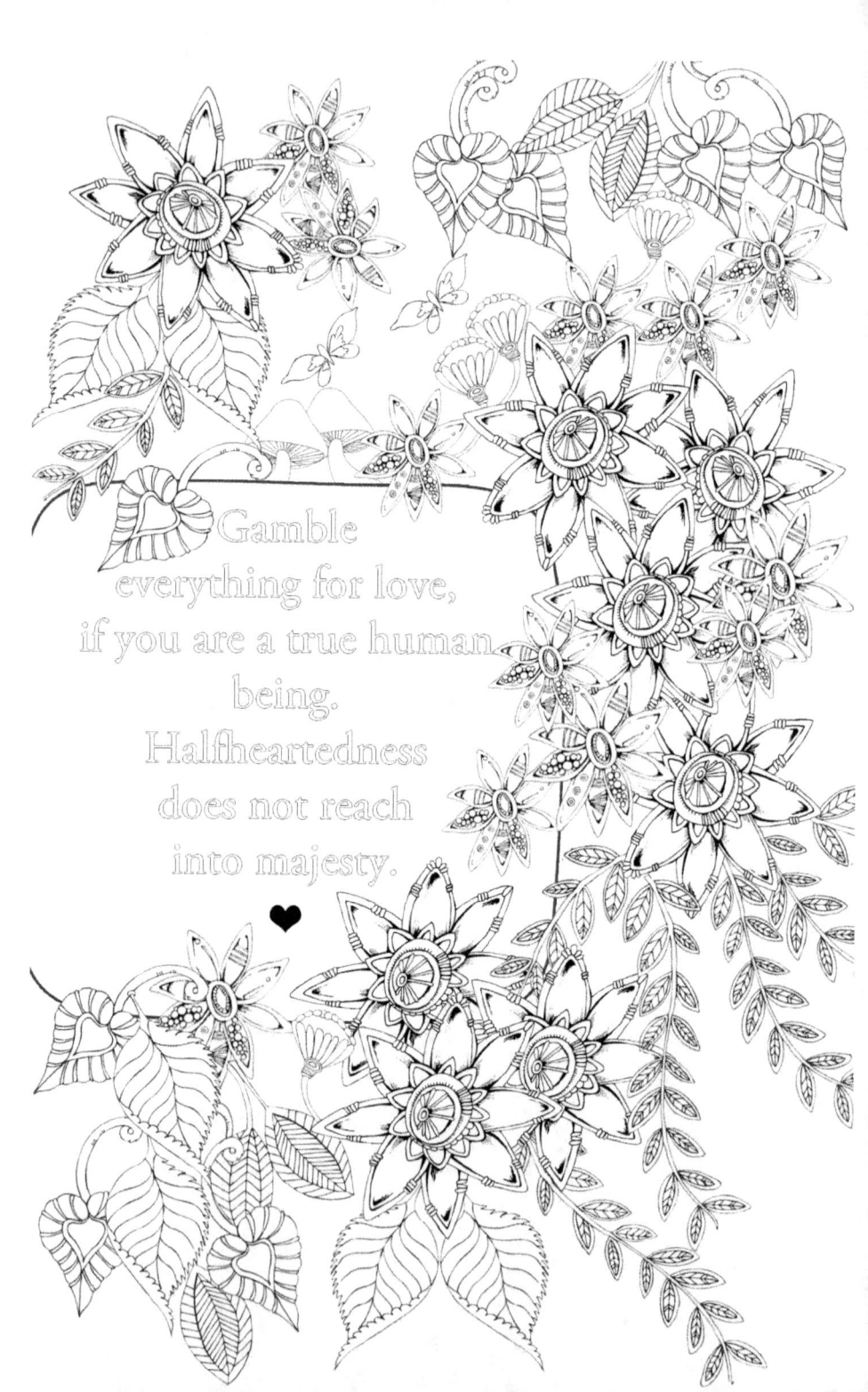

...
Rumi

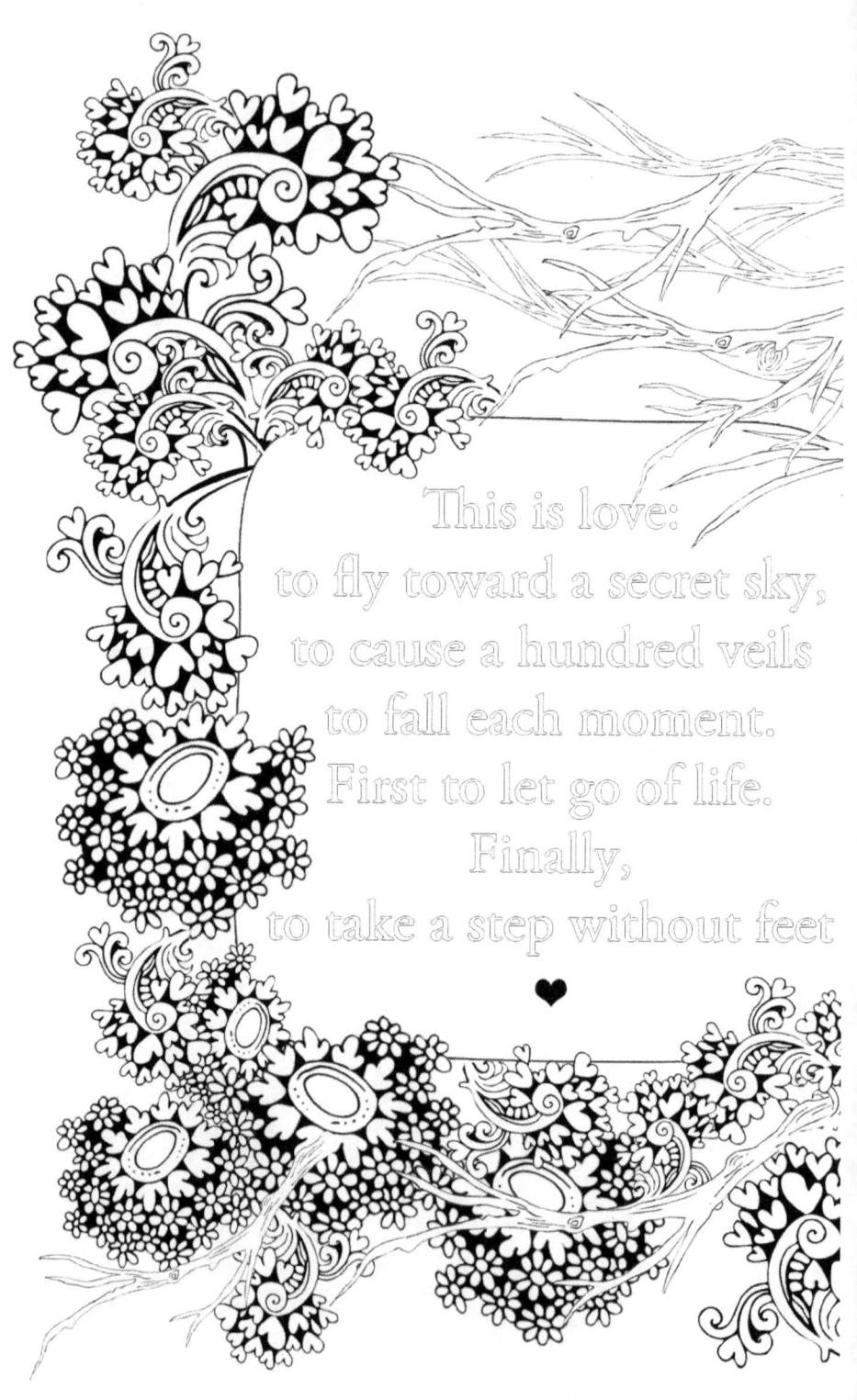

This is love:
to fly toward a secret sky,
to cause a hundred veils
to fall each moment.
First to let go of life.
Finally,
to take a step without feet.

...
Rumi

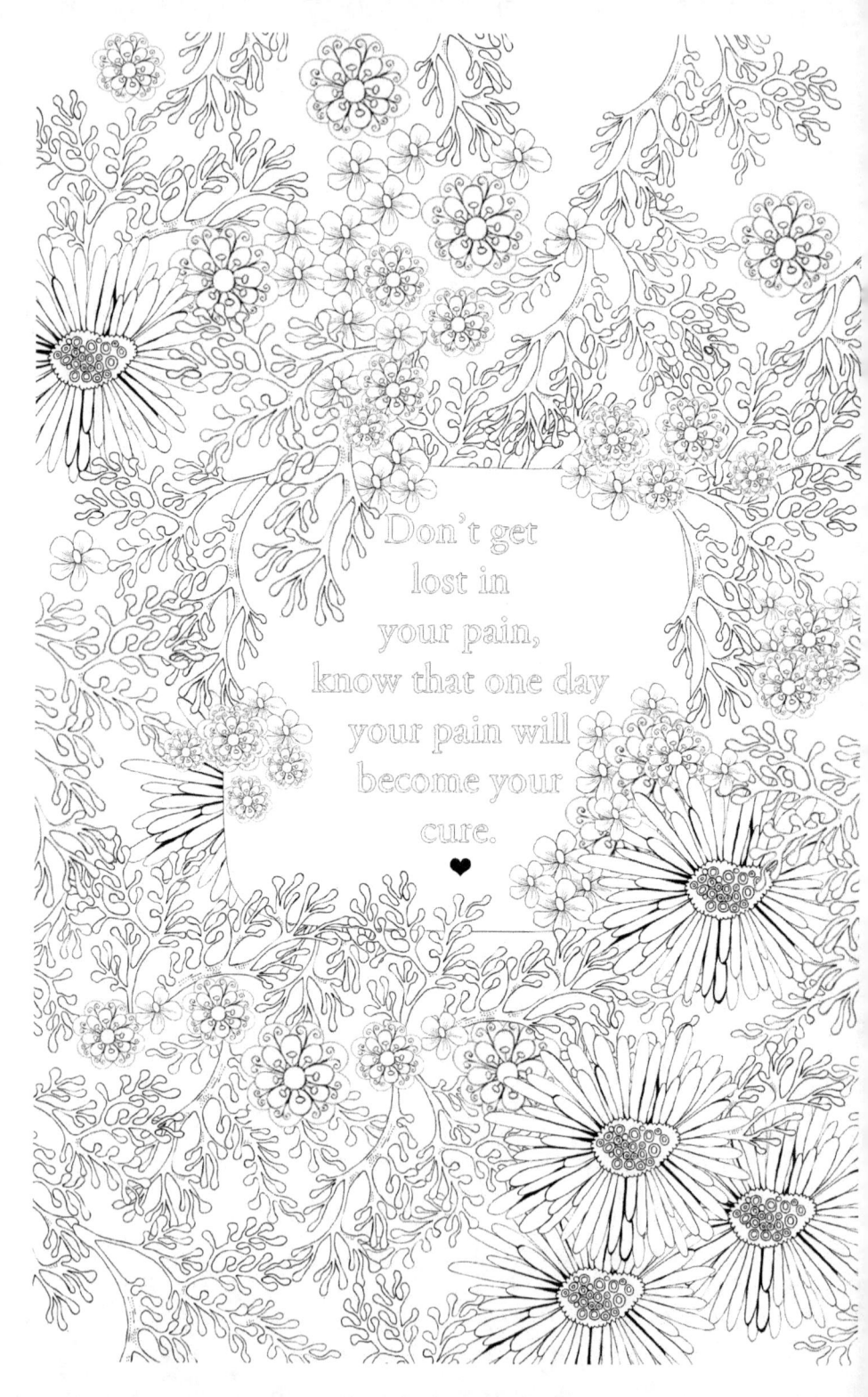

...
Rumi

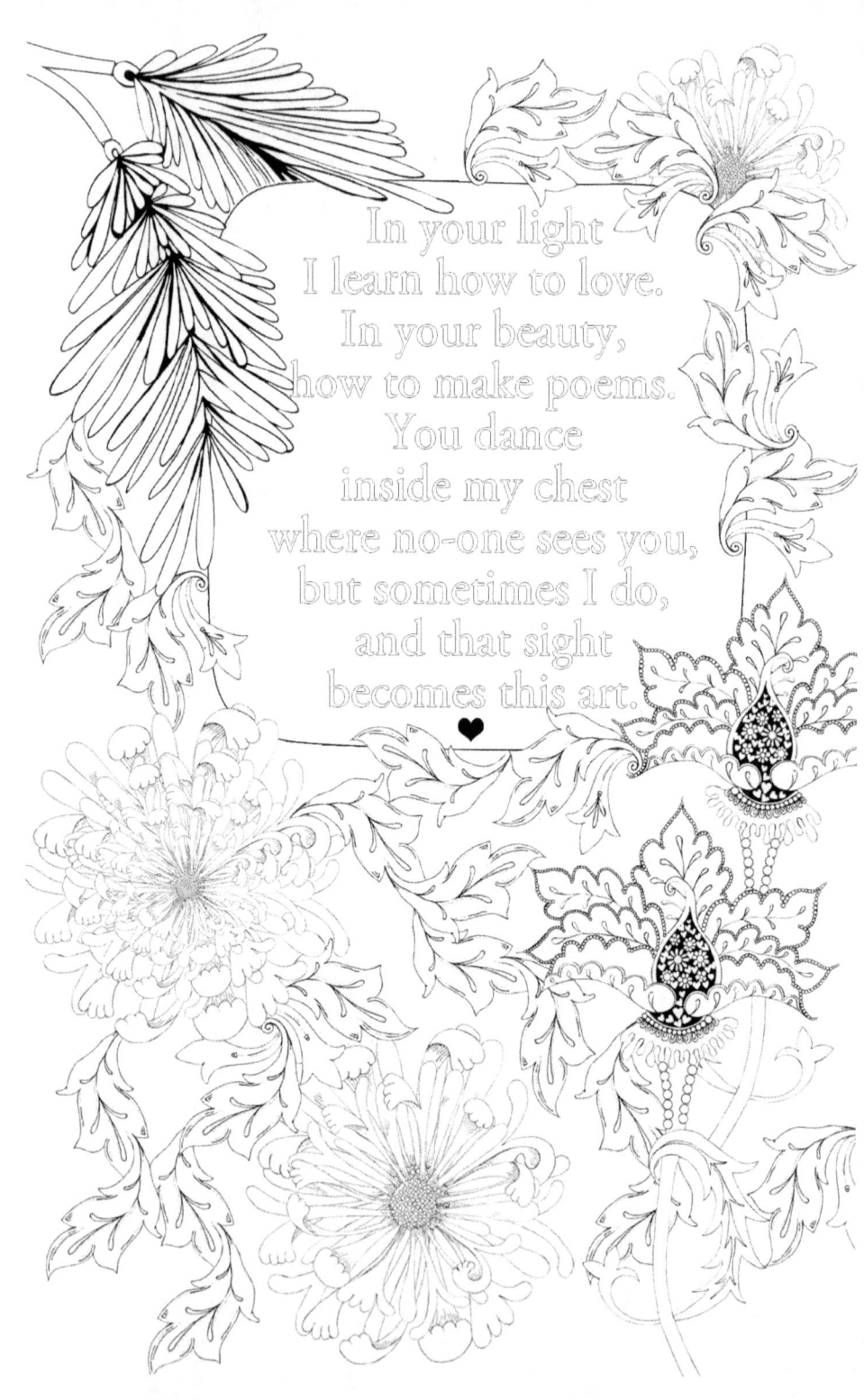

In your light
I learn how to love.
In your beauty,
how to make poems.
You dance
inside my chest
where no-one sees you,
but sometimes I do,
and that sight
becomes this art.

...
Rumi

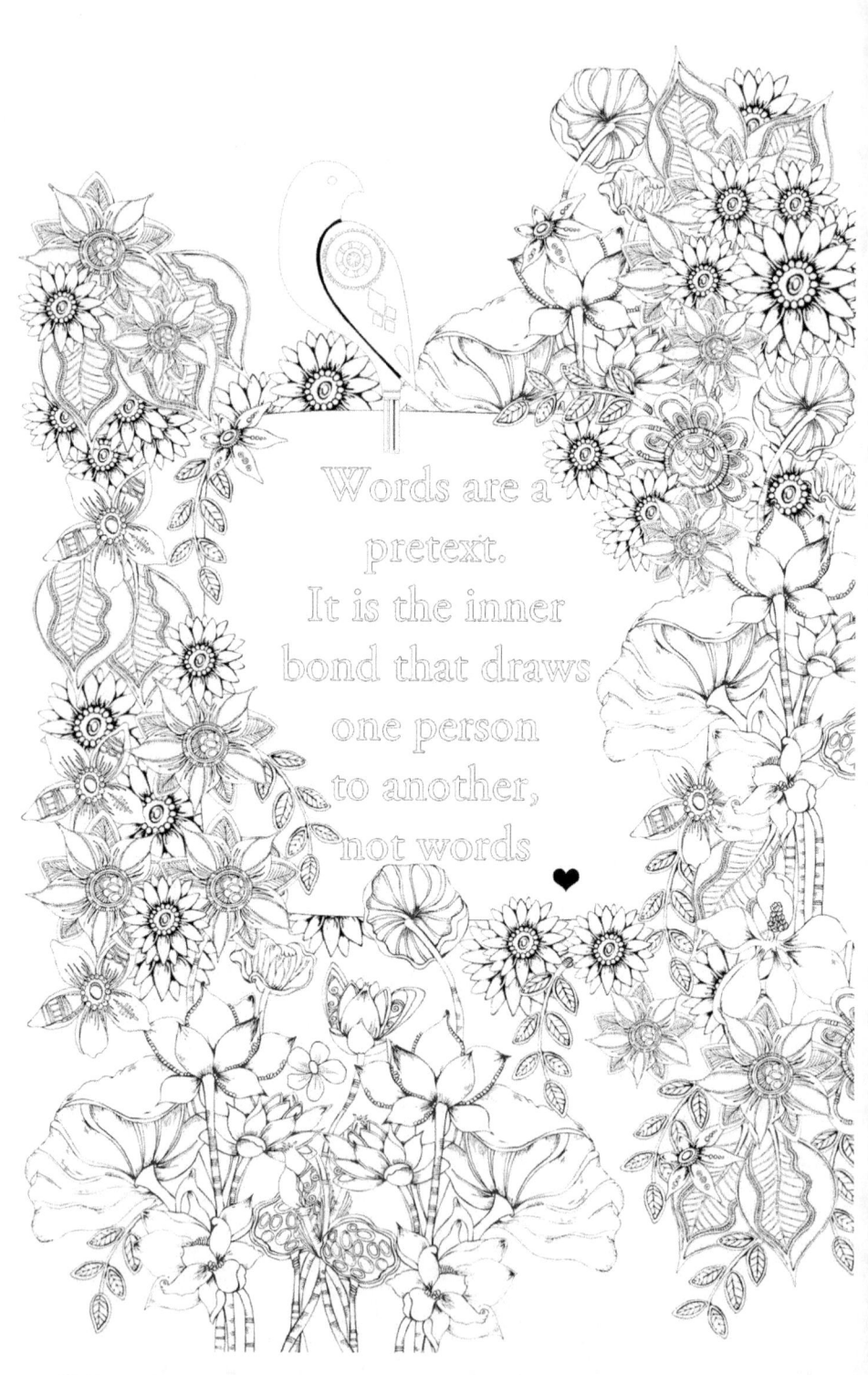

...
Rumi

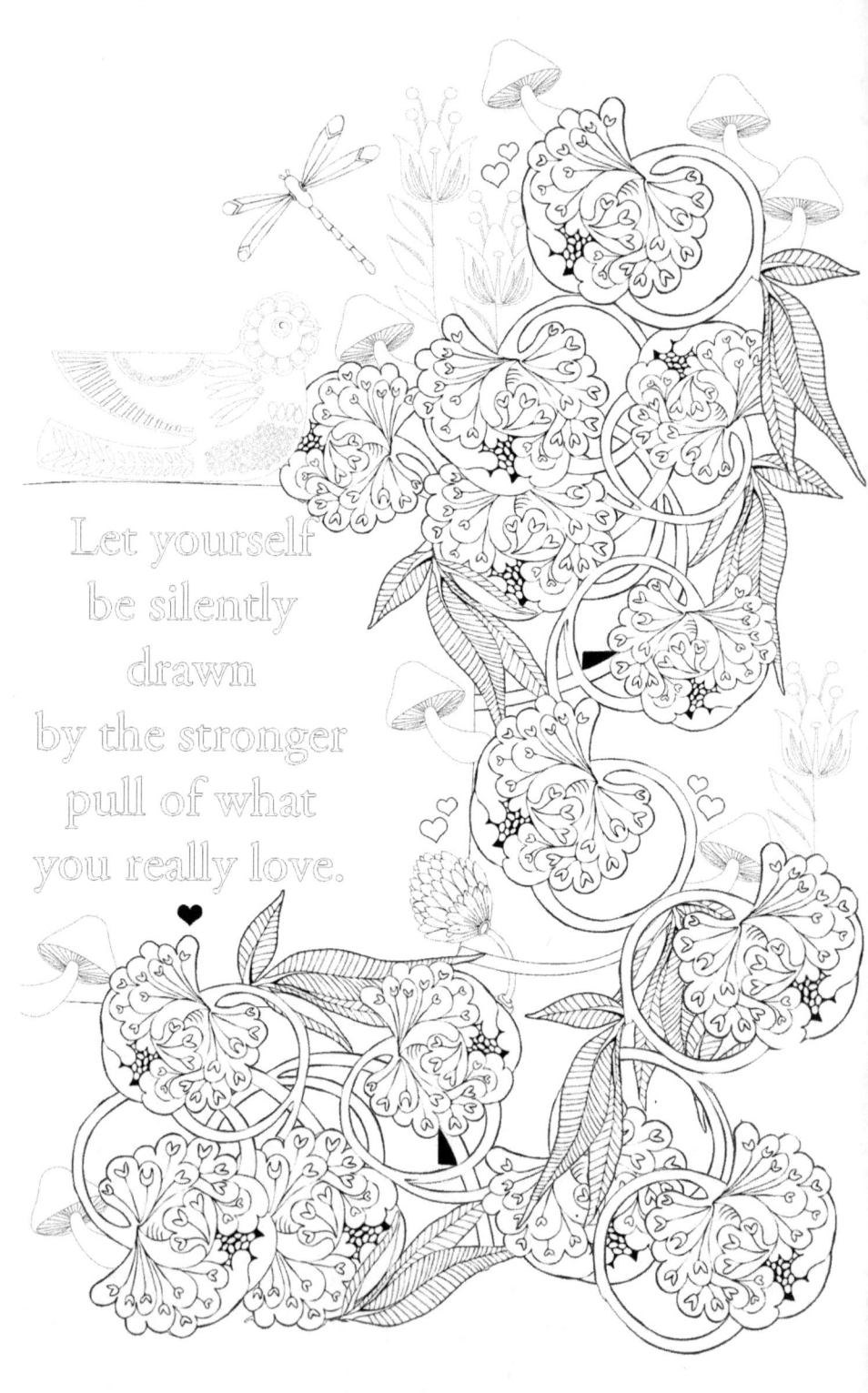

...
Rumi

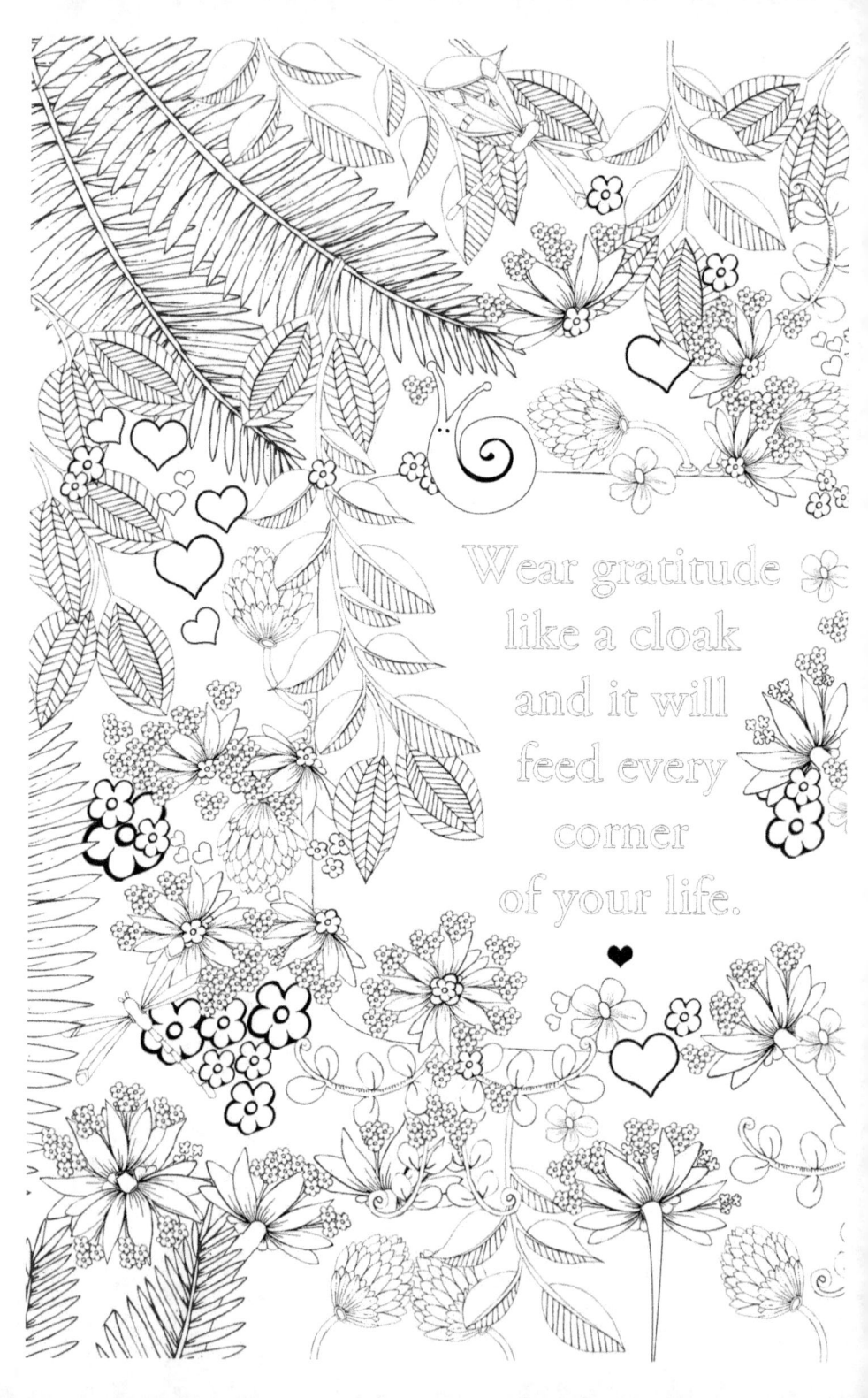

...
Rumi

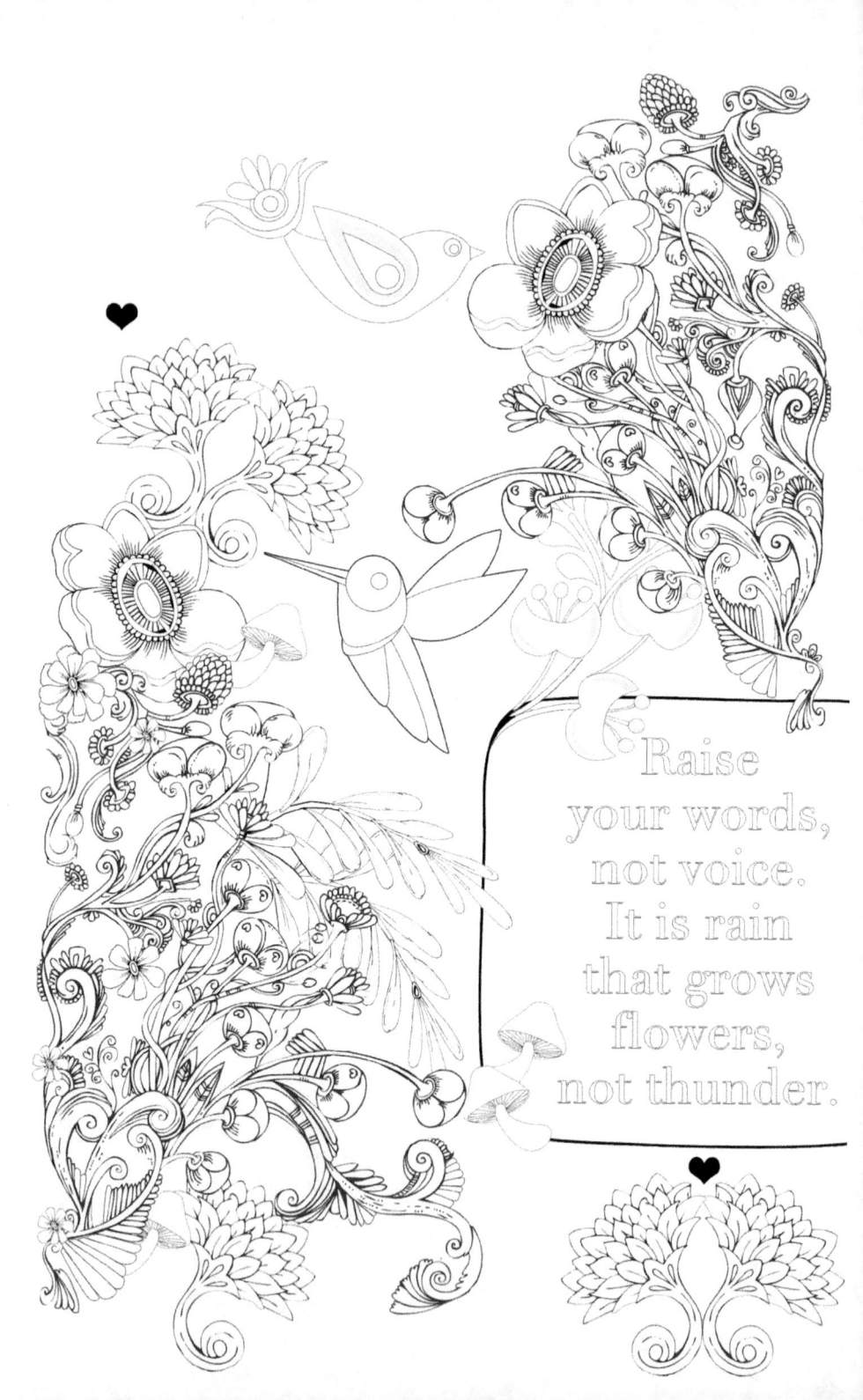

...
Rumi

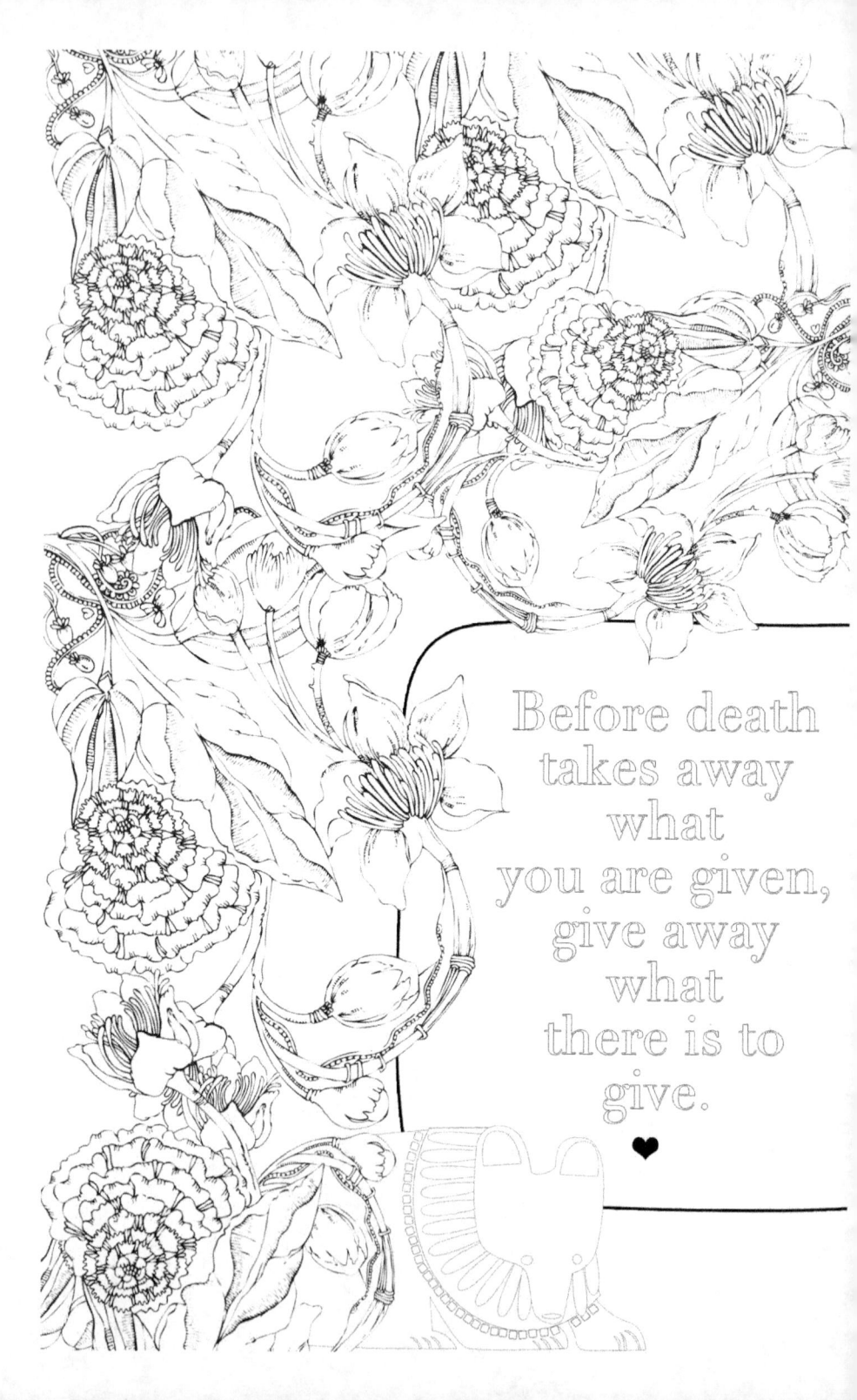

...
Rumi

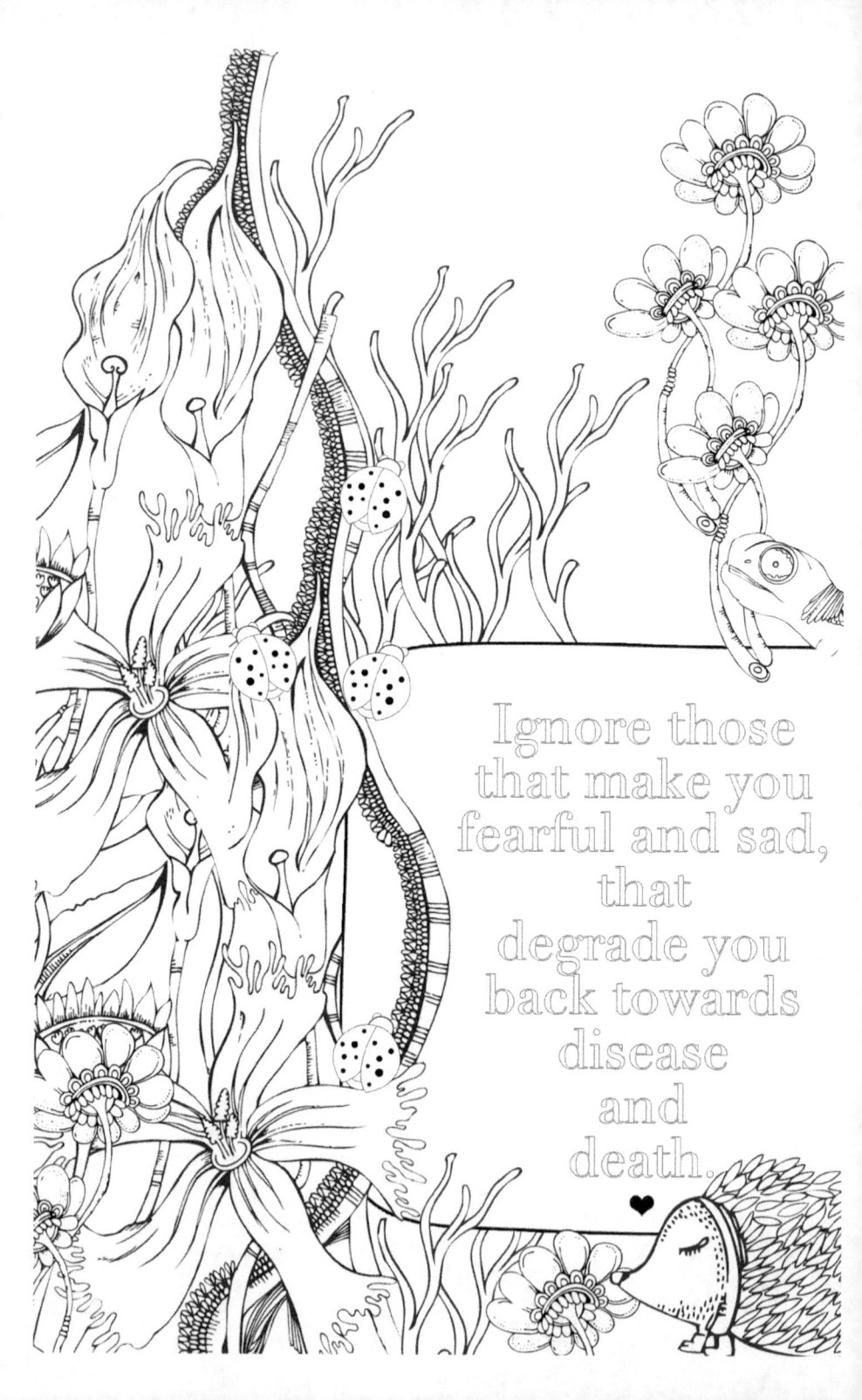

...
Rumi

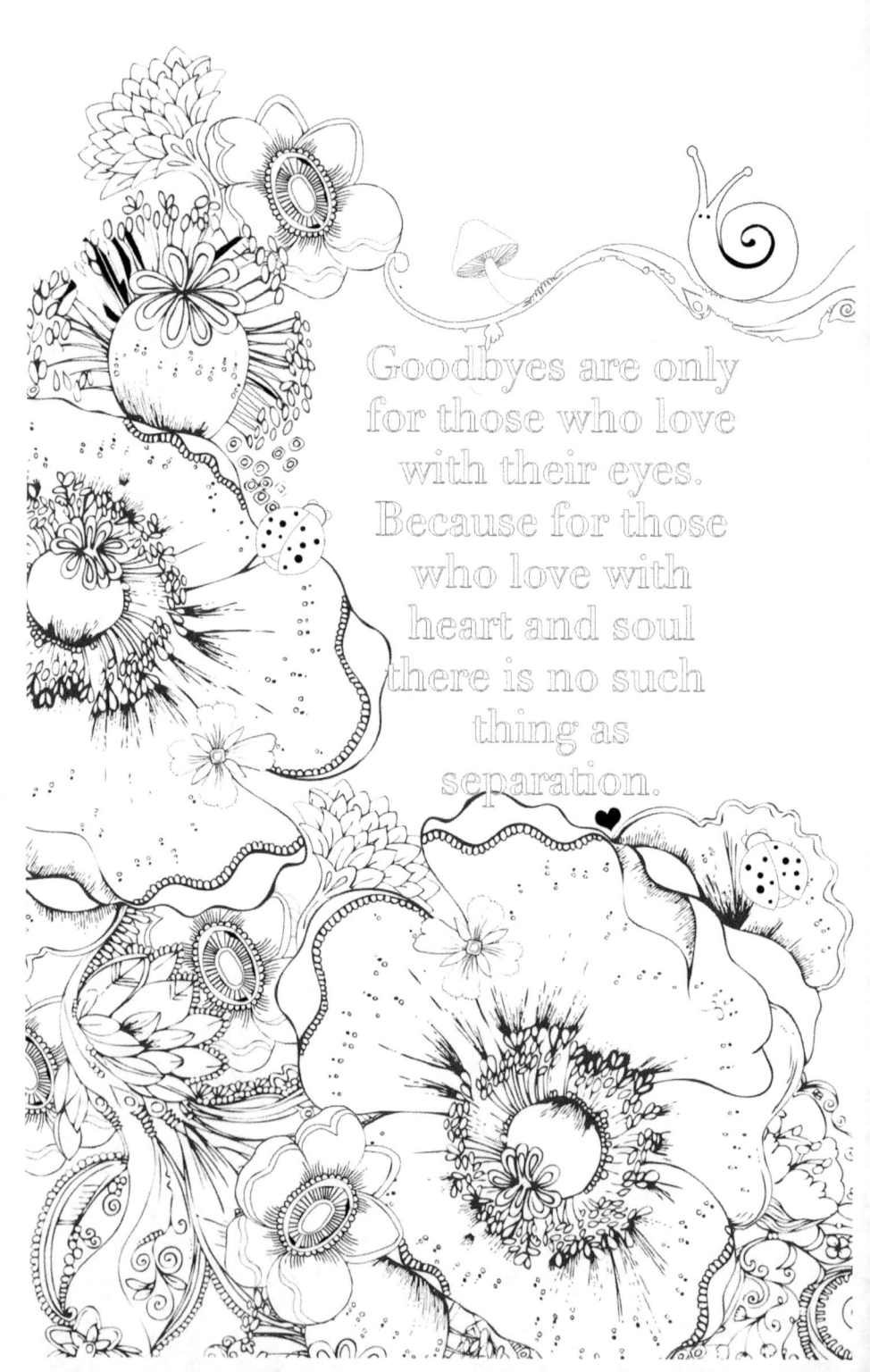

Rumi

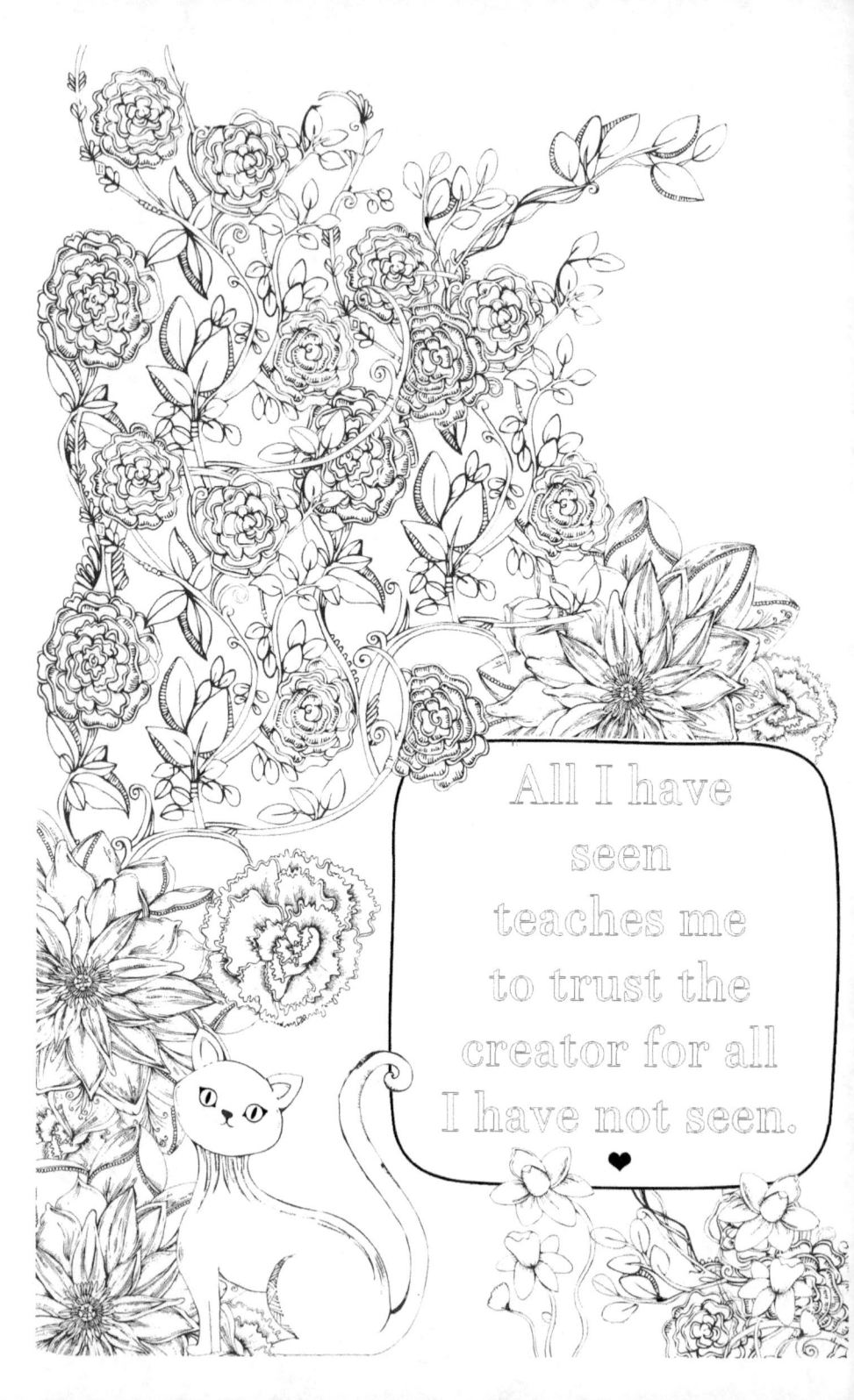

...
Rumi

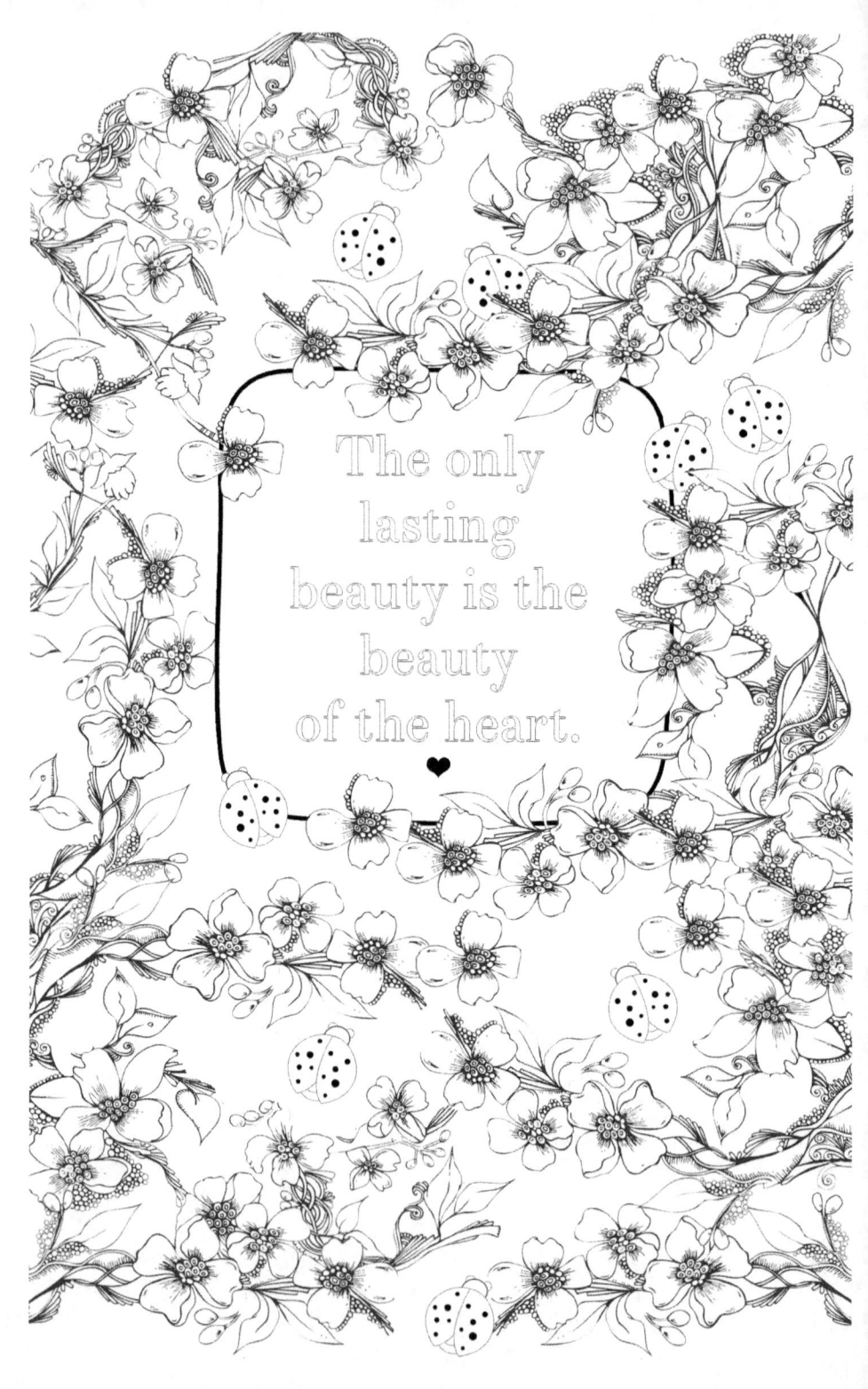

...
Rumi

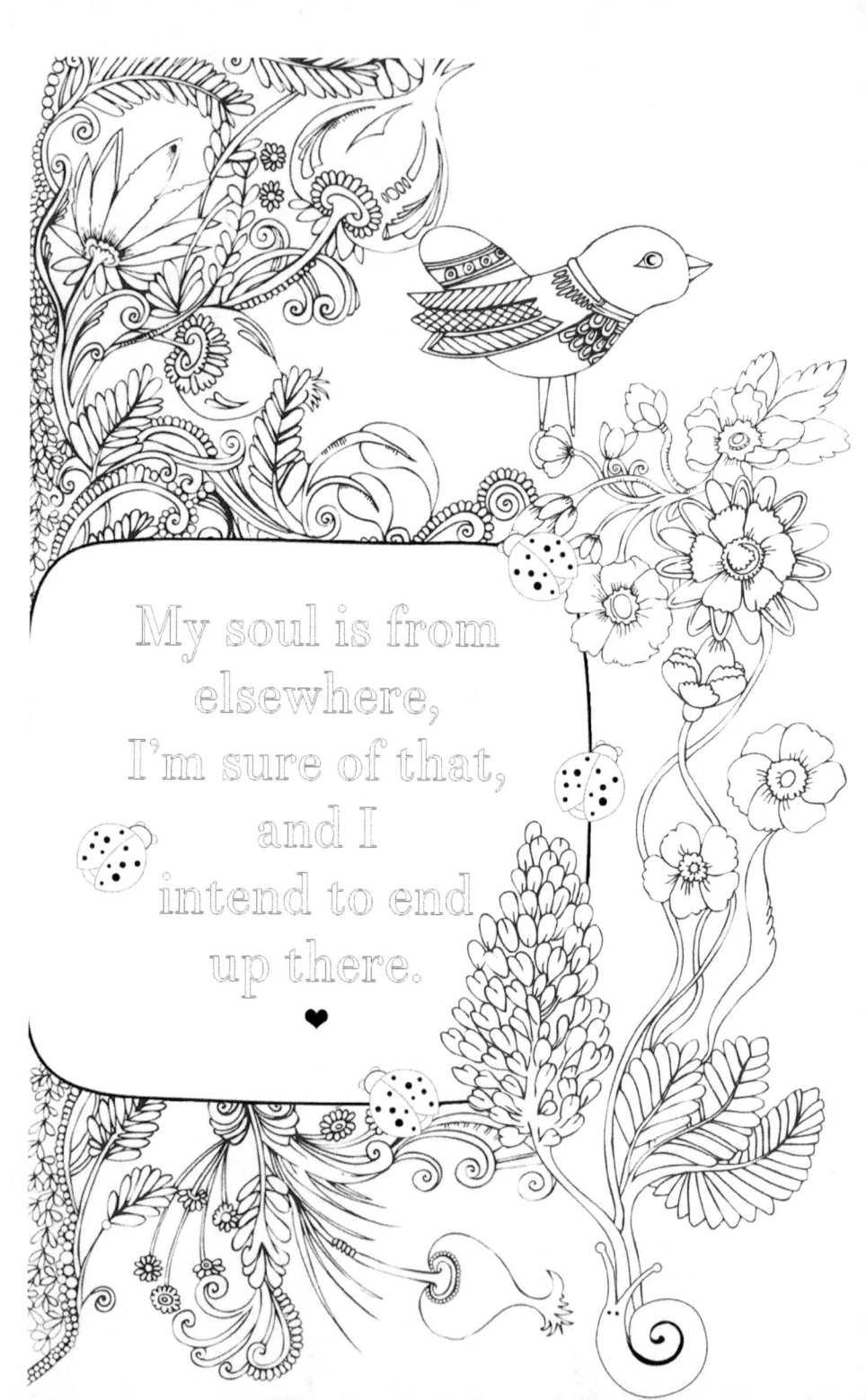

...
Rumi

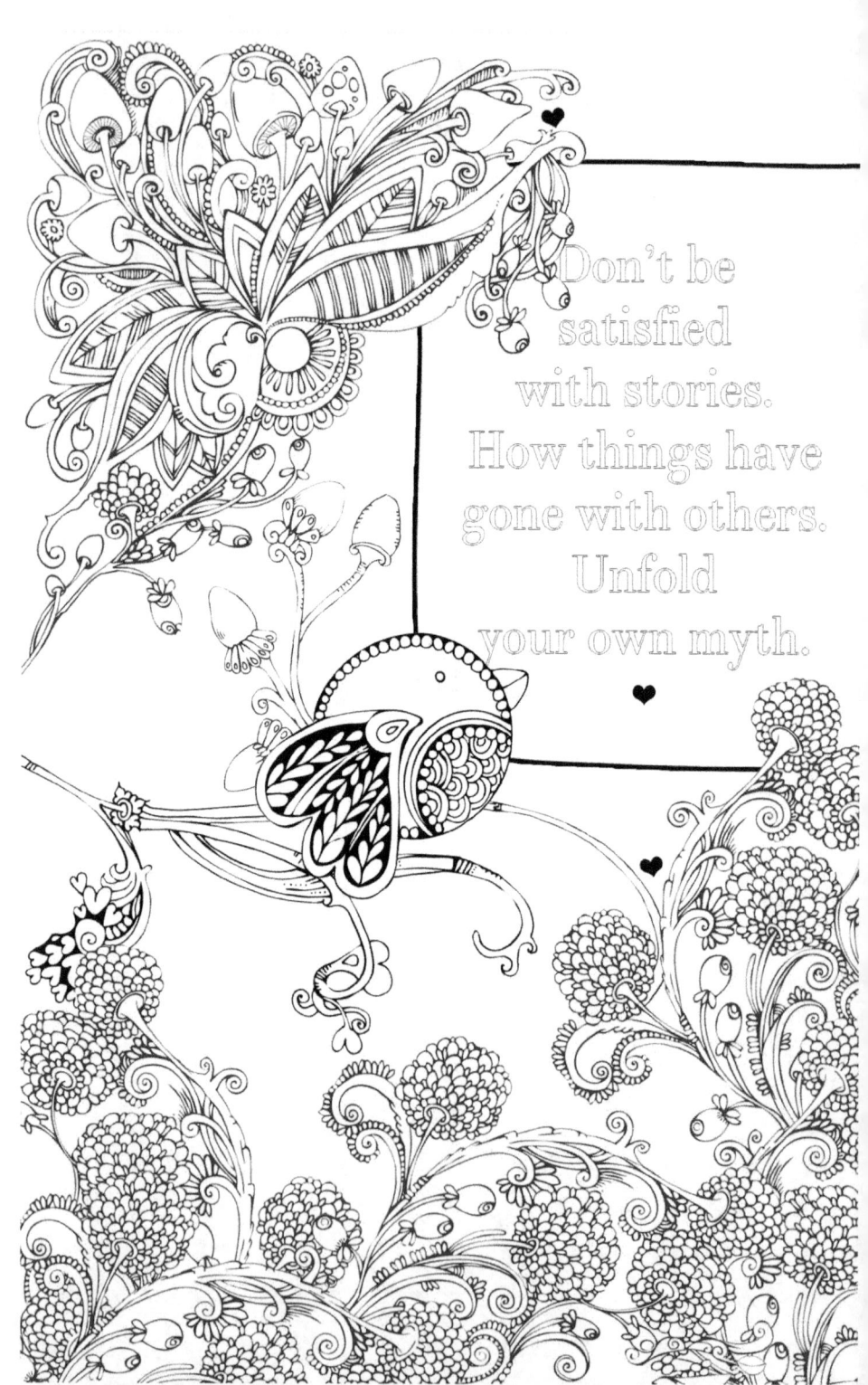

...
Rumi

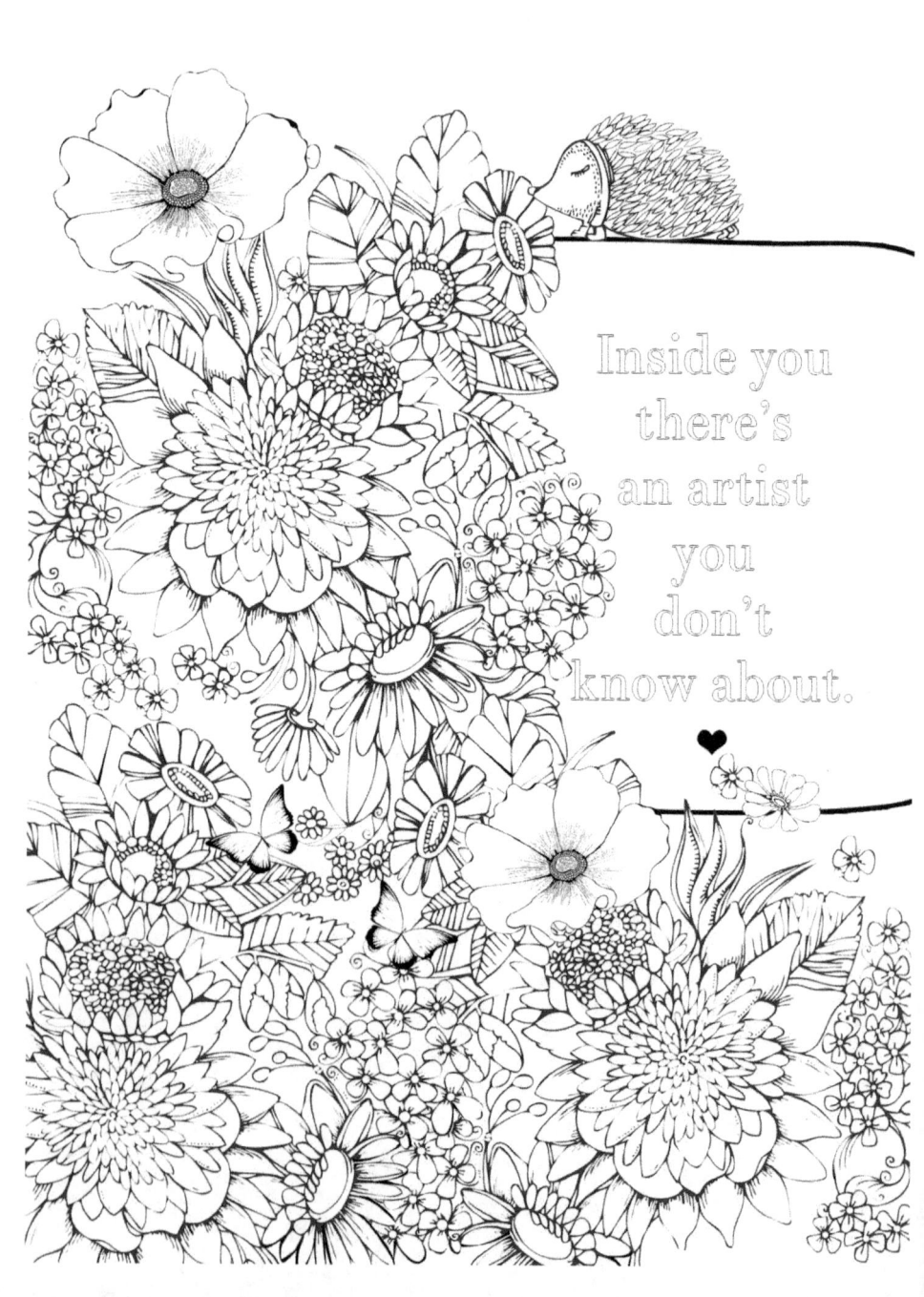

...
Rumi

When the world
pushes you
to your knees,
you're in the
perfect
position to pray.

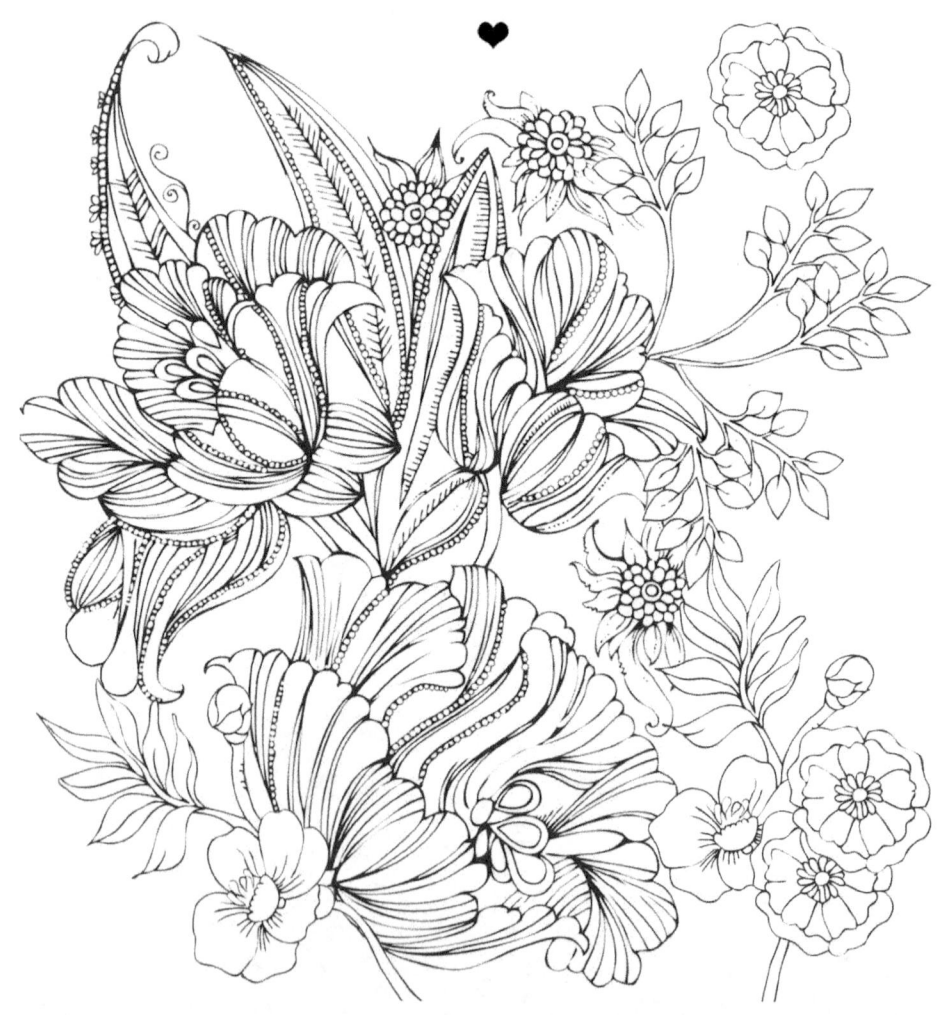

...
Rumi

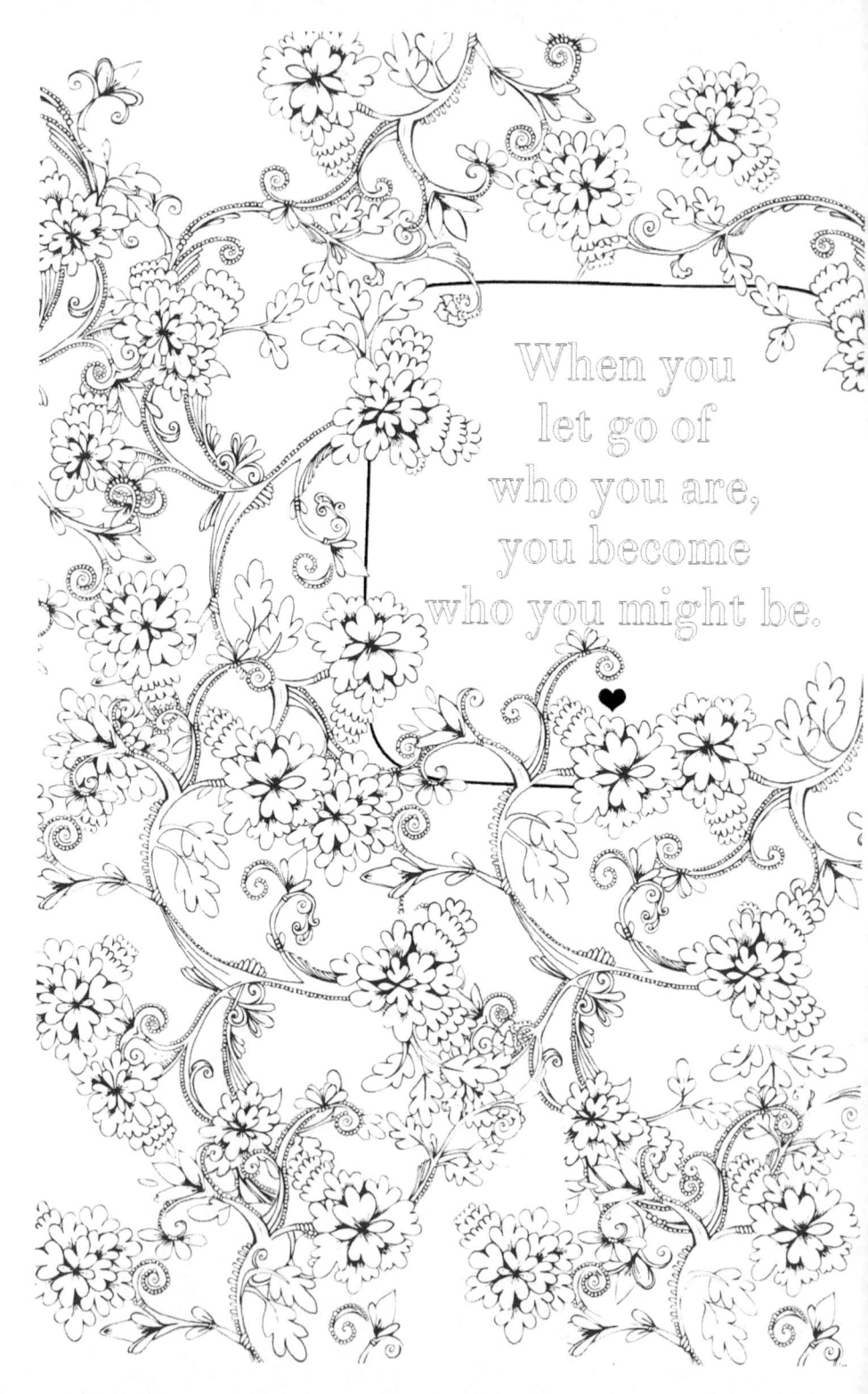

...
Rumi

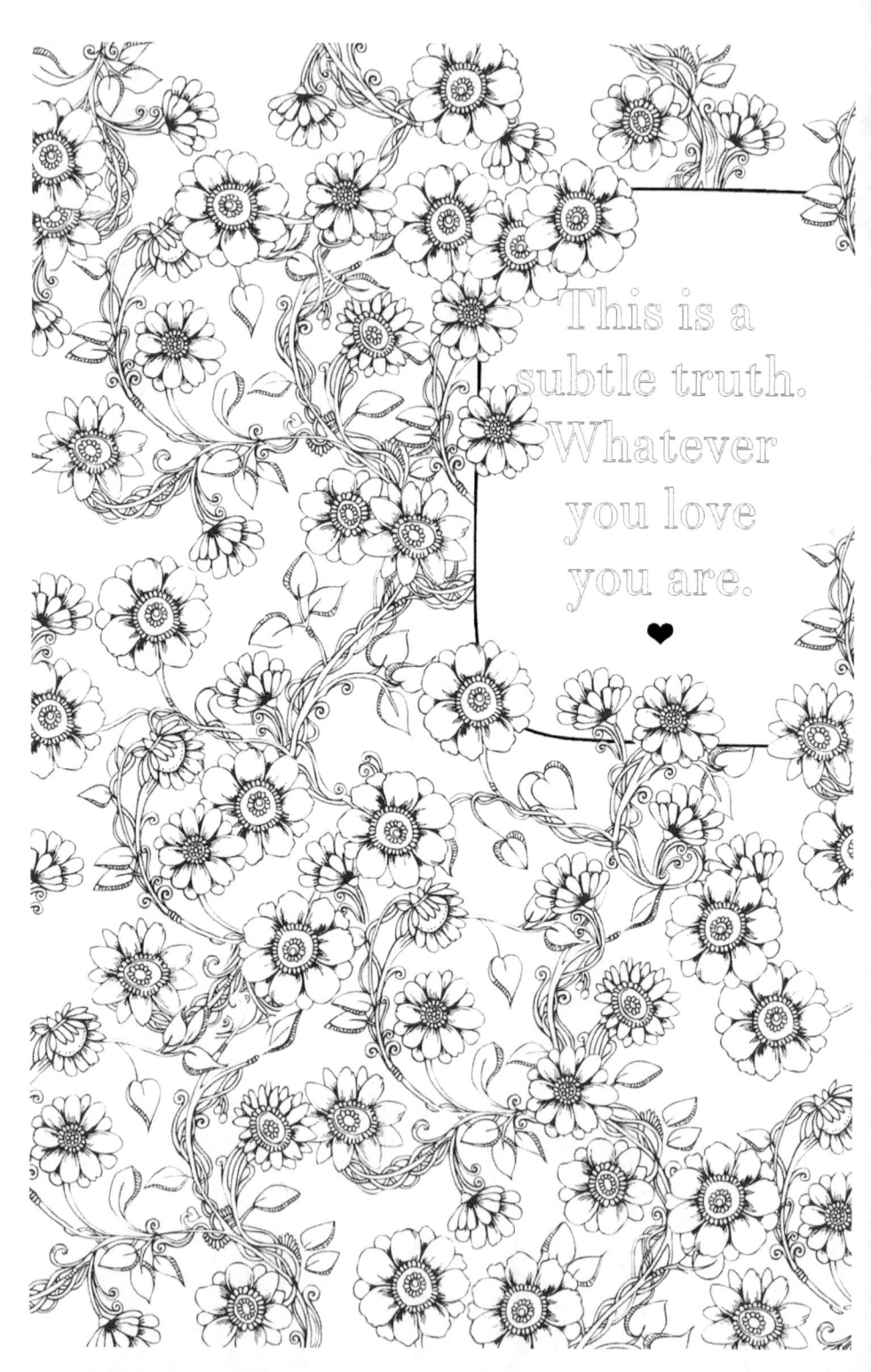

...
Rumi

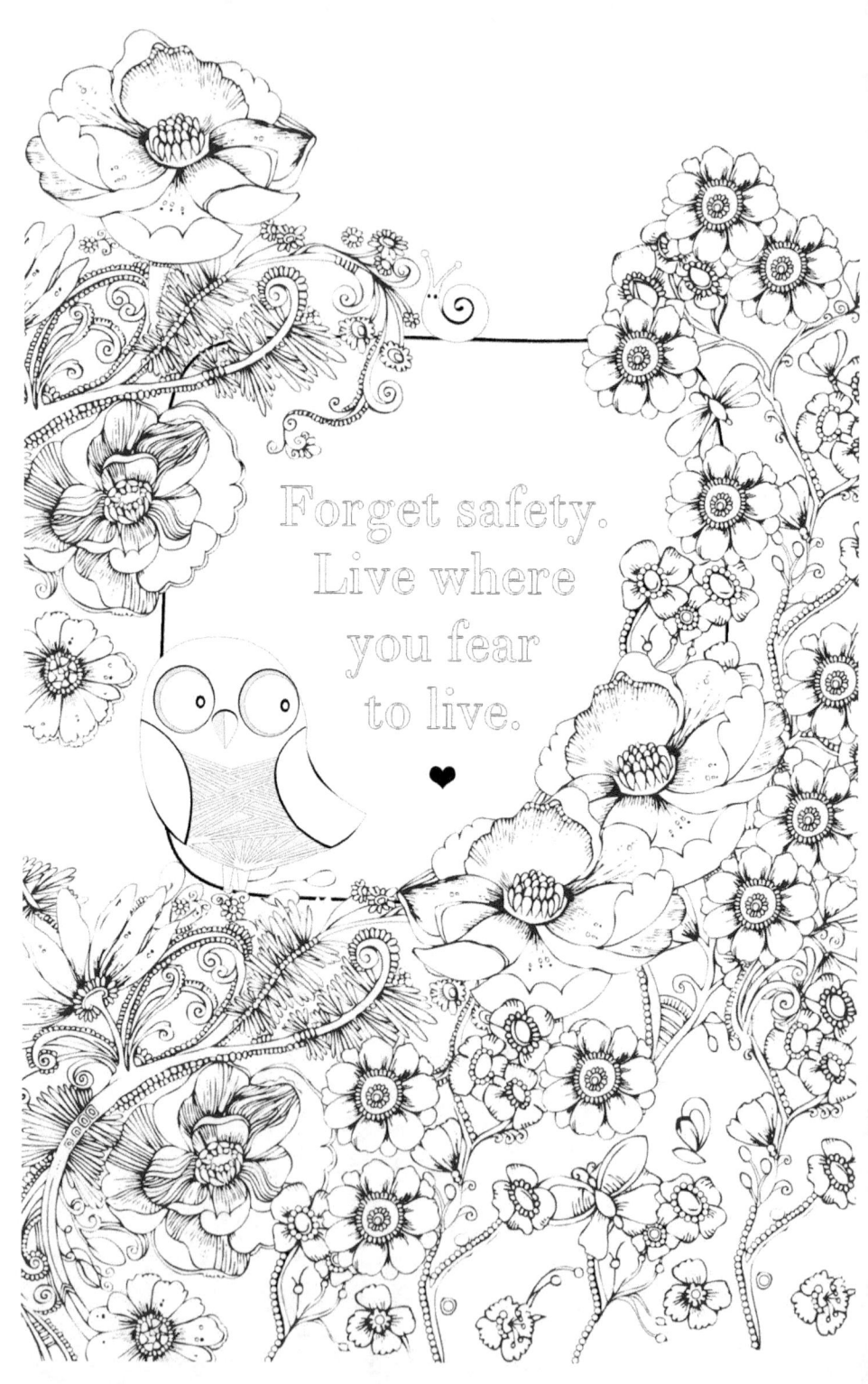

...
Rumi

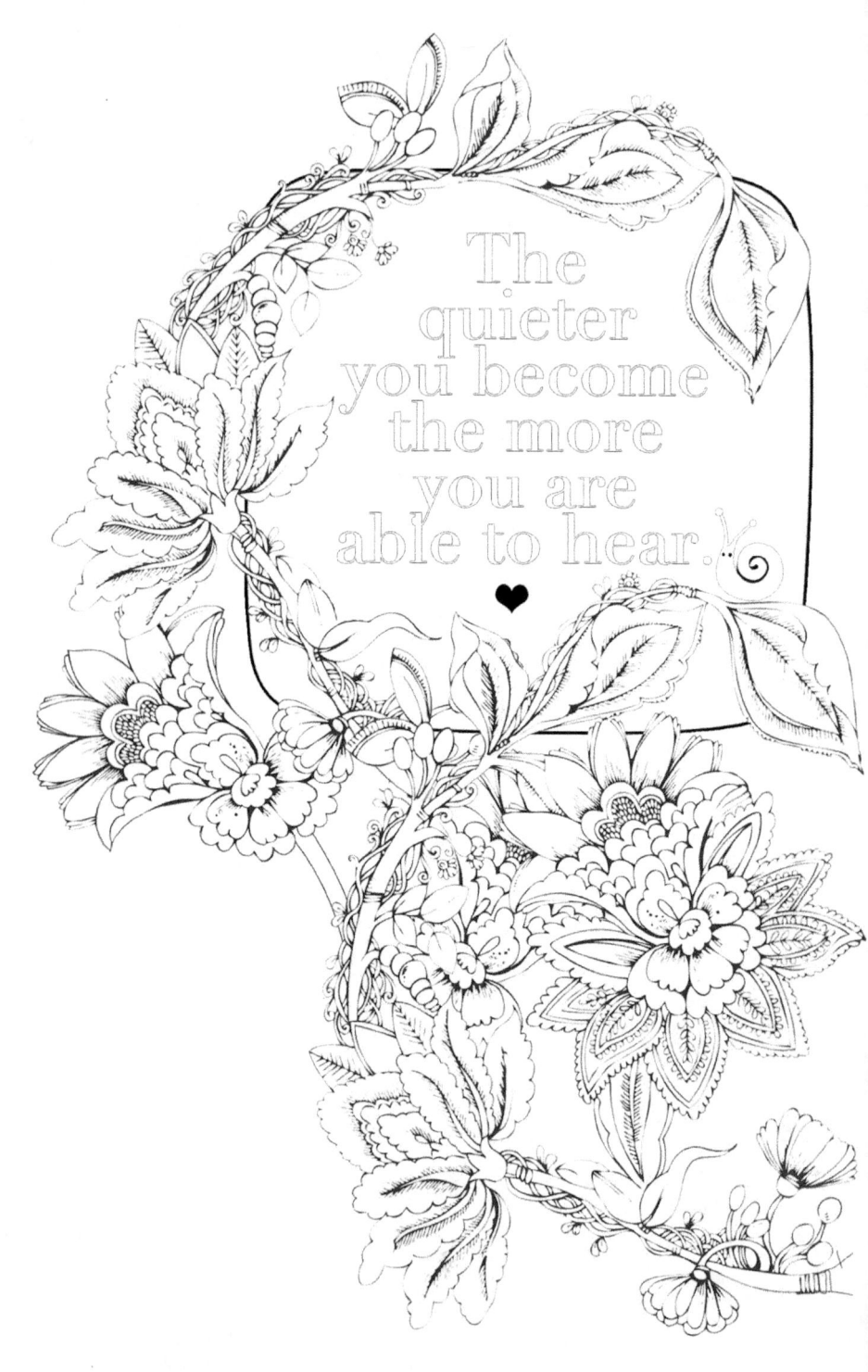

...
Rumi

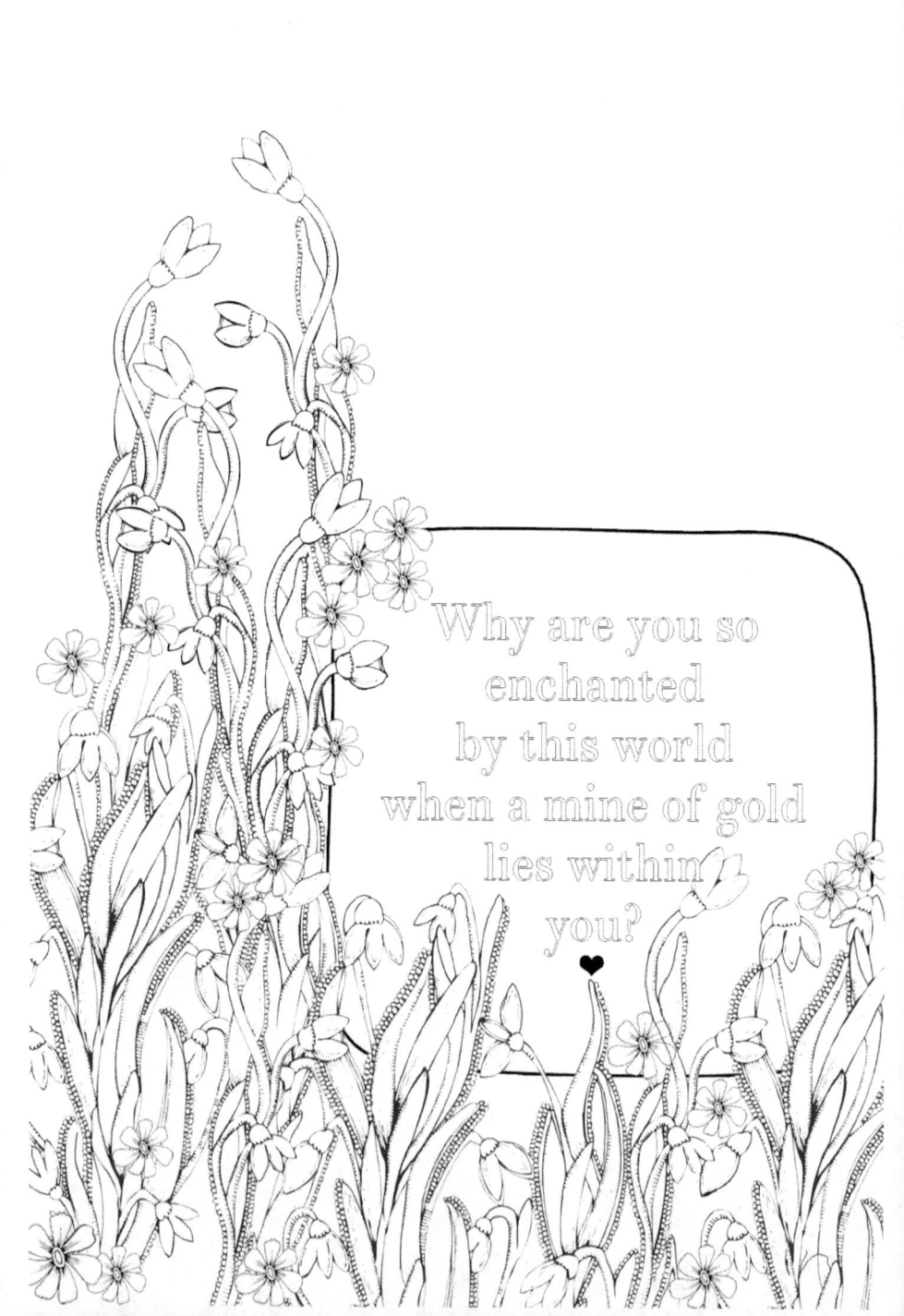